ONCE UPON
A RHYME

IMAGINATION FOR
A NEW GENERATION

. . . The End Of The Line
Vol III
Edited by Steve Twelvetree

 Young**Writers**

First published in Great Britain in 2005 by:
Young Writers
Remus House
Coltsfoot Drive
Peterborough
PE2 9JX
Telephone: 01733 890066
Website: www.youngwriters.co.uk

SB ISBN 1 84460 885 9

Foreword

Young Writers was established in 1991 and has been passionately devoted to the promotion of reading and writing in children and young adults ever since. The quest continues today. Young Writers remains as committed to engendering the fostering of burgeoning poetic and literary talent as ever.

This year's Young Writers competition has proven as vibrant and dynamic as ever and we are delighted to present a showcase of the best poetry from across the UK. Each poem has been carefully selected from a wealth of *Once Upon A Rhyme* entries before ultimately being published in this, our twelfth primary school poetry series.

Once again, we have been supremely impressed by the overall high quality of the entries we have received. The imagination, energy and creativity which has gone into each young writer's entry made choosing the best poems a challenging and often difficult but ultimately hugely rewarding task - the general high standard of the work submitted amply vindicating this opportunity to bring their poetry to a larger appreciative audience.

We sincerely hope you are pleased with our final selection and that you will enjoy *Once Upon A Rhyme . . . The End Of The Line Vol III* for many years to come.

Contents

Shaun Nazir (10)	24
Joshua Monaghan (9)	24
Dale Storry (10)	25
Jordan Hugill (10)	26
Abby Underwood (9)	27
Bethany Wrafter (10)	28

Brooke Hill School, Oakham

Mary Leefe (9)	28
Leah Edmonston (10)	29
Charlie Dearden (10)	29
Daisy Crump (10)	30
Martha Clewlow (9)	31
Georgina Baker (10)	32
Holli Munford (10)	32
Jamie Williamson (11)	33
Hannah Elthorpe (9)	33
Amy Carter (10)	34
Aaron Roy (9)	34
Emily Bailey (11)	35
Emma Williams (10)	35

Chapel Primary School, Chapel-en-le-Frith

Asher Oliver (7)	36
Rebecca Green (7)	36
Martyn Bonham (7)	37
Adam Barnes (7)	37
Benjamin Hall (7)	38
Rebecca Ryan (7)	38
Thomas Anderson (7)	38
Fiona Biggin (7)	39
George Buxton	39
Bethanie Williamson (10)	40

Christ The King Catholic Junior School, Coundon

Cian Kavanagh (8)	40
Danielle Friel (8)	40
Natasha Rollason (8)	41
Sean Cavigan (8)	41
Emily Holland (8)	41
Christie O'Toole (8)	42

Eleanor McKeown (8)   42
Elissa Sheehan (8)   43
James Mohan (8)   43
Sarah Molloy (8)   44
Lydia Black (8)   44
Christopher Kelly (8)   45
Caitlin Reidy (8)   45
Charlotte Evatt (8)   45

Coppull Parish Church School, Coppull
Laoura Parginou (11)   46
Laura Wareing (10)   46
Cameron Sharratt   47
Liam Mutch (10)   47
Rianne Holme (11)   48
Adam Bennett (10)   49
Shaun Greenhalgh (11)   50
Alex Winward (10)   50
Jonathon South (10)   51
Joe David Squires (10)   51
Gemma Coulthard (10)   52
Jean Penney (10)   52
Michael Ian Thomas (10)   53
Michael Tasker (11)   53
Abbigail Meegan (10)   54
Katie McNamara (11)   54
Alice Bury (10)   55
Rebecca Bradley (10)   56
Nathan Bennett (10)   57
Andy Holme (11)   58
Claudia Westhead (10)   59
Emily Borrowdale (10)   60

Crossflatts Primary School, Crossflatts
Poppy Jane Bellerby (8)   60
Bethanie Dunning (9)   61
Laura Foy (8)   61
Benjamin Whitfield (8)   61
Ellie Morris (7)   62
Lauren Corby (8)   62
Elliott Bedford (8)   63

Lauren Calvert (8)	63
Lauren John (7)	64
Hollie Whitford (8)	64
Aaron Lee Tscherniga (7)	65
Sam Bone (7)	65
Hannah Foy (8)	66
Lauren Benson (7)	67

Eastcroft Park CP School, Knowsley
Bekki Carragher (10)	67
Carl Evans (11)	68
Kellie Carragher (9)	68

East Stanley School, East Stanley
| Helen Greaves (9) | 69 |
| Nathan Brown (9) | 69 |

Eton Wick CE First School, Eton Wick
Alice Fletcher (8)	70
Georgia McGlasson (7)	70
Stanley Clifford (7)	70
Eleanor O'Donnell (8)	71
Hannah Davies (7)	71
Charlotte Bone (7)	71
Bethany Taylor (8)	72
Daniel George Morgan (8)	72
Jake Church (7)	73
Rebecca Blair (7)	73
Humair Munawer (7)	73
Jack Steptoe (7)	74
Roopinder Virdee (7)	74
Gaganpreet Chana (8)	74
Gaganpreet Chana & Alice Fletcher (8)	75

Fosse Primary School, Leicester
Remi Georgallis (11)	75
Lucy Louise Crisp (10)	76
Liam Smith (9)	76
Charlotte Louise Gallagher (10)	77
Cherish Dean (10)	77

Jorden Deannan Fox (11)	78
Catherine Peach (10)	78
Rhian Ward (10)	79
Thomas Simpson (10)	79
Muhammad Bhawoodin (9)	79
Sarata Seisay (10)	80
Thomas Arrowsmith (9)	80
Berwick Dawson (9)	81
Tapiwa Savanhu (10)	81
Katie Allen (9)	81
Tyler West (10)	82
Katie Louise Walton Barnes (9)	82
Roísìn Murphy (9)	83
Paris Parra-Watson (10)	83
Ashleigh Giles (10)	83

Foxes Piece School, Marlow

Liam Murray	84
Daniel Page (8)	84
Victoria Mundy	84
Kirsty Walsh (8)	85
Rosie Edmonds	85
Caroline Hester (9)	85
Tamara Comley (8)	86
Kiri Hall	86
Michael Sproate (8)	86
Lauren Taylor (8)	87
Amber Moore	87
Frank Alderman (8)	87
Josh Dean (8)	88
Billie Burns	88
Annabel Ogden (8)	88
Shane Wyatt (7)	89
Sophie Giles	89
Emma-Louise Foster (10)	89
Ashley Dean (10)	90
Kelly Buck (11)	90
Ka-Ho Chan (11)	90
Jamie Jones	91
Hannah Page (10)	91
Adam Newson	91

Corrina Bignall	92
Harry Elliman	92
Ben Newson	92
Mitzi Settle	93
Laila Lanigan	93
Chloe Ball (10)	93
Matthew Tipping	94
Jasmine Power (10)	94
Daniel Moore (10)	94
Michael Ogden (10)	95
Harry Norton (10)	95
Aislinn Darvell (9)	95
Georgina Harper (9)	96
Patrick Castle (9)	96
Sayma Rob (10)	96
Esther Williams (10)	97
Jack Smith	97
Harry Scrace	97
Dominic Lai	98
Ashley Lanigan	98
Georgina Giles	98
Ryan Haas (8)	99
Rebecca Jones	99
Summayyah Shah (7)	99
Chantelle Bennett (8)	100
Leanne Dix	100
Danielle Lovett (7)	100
Perri Miller	101
Connor Bignall	101
Jessica Hunter (8)	101

Gig Mill Primary School, Stourbridge

Roisin Flannery (10)	102
Mairead Flannery (8)	102

Gilberdyke Primary School, Gilberdyke

Tonicha Massam (6)	103

Grayshott CE Primary School, Hindhead

Abigail Jackson (9)	103
Shona Morrison (10)	104

Rebecca Plant (8)	184
Jodie Highfield (8)	185
Jamie Bowen (9)	185
Jaspreet Kaur Japper (9)	185
Holly Taylor (10)	186
Aidan Lewis (8)	186
Holly Lennard (10)	187
Jake Cox (9)	187
Lauren Potts (8)	188
Joseph James (8)	188
Jamie Haynes (10)	188
Sasha Perry (8)	189
Heather Cockfield (10)	189
Emily Callaghan (9)	189
Ravinder Gill (8)	190
Emy Brown (9)	191
Max Sheffield (9)	191
Rhianne Springthorpe (10)	192
Sarah Whitehouse (8)	192
Shannon Luck (10)	193
Rebecca Robinson (8)	193
Stephanie Jones (9)	194
Sasha Cox (8)	194
Charlotte Howell (9)	195
Daniel Sowinski (10)	195
Baljinder Sondh (10)	196
Glen Reece (9)	196
Ethan Westwood (8)	197
Adam Cooke (8)	197

Townsend Primary School, London

Lewis Martins (10)	198
Holly Flynn (8)	198
Halima Brown (9)	199
Oliver O'Connor (10)	199
Ashley Atkin (10)	200
Haja Sesay (10)	200
Kelly Thomas (10)	201

Trinity CE VA First School, Verwood

Westbourne Primary School, Westbourne

William Patten School, London

The Poems

White Beard

Did you hear? Did you know?
There he comes like a black crow
A pirate called White Beard
And at the king's face, he sneered.

Did you hear? Did you see?
When White Beard ruled the sea
Drinking beer and rum as he went
Swearing never to repent.

Did you hear? Did you talk?
When the king's face was like chalk
The great navy was called to arms
The emperor did raise the alarm.

Did you hear? Did you tell?
When the sea turned to Hell
The navy's cannons gave a mighty roar
And White Beard was seen no more.

Paul Adams

Home From School

Seeing my front door when I get out of my car.
Seeing my mum cooking my tea.
Seeing my special pets.
Seeing my grubby friend.
Hearing my TV rattling on.
Hearing my mum say hello to me.
Hearing my door handle creak and creak.
Tasting my beautiful dinner.
Tasting the beautiful drink go down my long neck.
Tasting my lovely Pot Noodle.
Touching my sofa as I walk in my lounge.
Touching and cuddling my mum.

Hollie Delaney (9)

Animal Alphabet

A lbatross bite you,
B aboons swing at you,
C ats scram you,
D ogs bark at you,
E agles peck you,
F ish spit at you,
G orillas poop at you,
H ares pull your hairs off,
I guanas whack their tails at you,
J ellyfish poison you,
K angaroos jump on you,
L ions roar at you,
M onkeys chuck food at you,
N ewts crawl on you,
O strich peck you,
P igs shoot mud at you,
Q uails fly at you,
R hinos kill you,
S nakes hiss at you,
T igers crawl at you,
U nicorns smile at you,
V ulcan are nasty to you,
W alrus dig their tusks at you,
X is a secret,
Y aks bite you,
Z ebras show their stripes at you.

Joel Wayne-Morris

The Wind Can Be . . .

The wind can be powerful,
The wind can go *crash!*
The wind can be furious,
The wind can go *bash!*

Rachel Hodges (8)

My Older Sister

I have an older sister,
She is growing up very fast,
I don't want her to grow up,
I just want her childhood to last!

She won't play games with me anymore,
She won't run and play,
She will sit up in her room
And watch TV *all day!*

If only she were more active
To keep me company
So I could be much happier
As she'd be playing with me!

I really do still love her
Although she isn't fun
All you can do is move on
And say 'What's done is done!'

Annabelle Hernaman (11)

Summer

Summer is here, as bright as can be
I go out and play with she, who's me
I feel the summer's breeze on my lonely feet
I play all day
Near the summer's bay
My friends come to me,
To see how I be
My mother says to me, 'Get in!' see
I'm locked inside, it feels like prison looking outside
My friends and I together, side by side
The trees so very still
I feel like I am on a hill
All the children playing outside
Except for me, who's lonely as a cloud!

Miski Ahmed (11)

My Family

My sister is mad,
And my brother is too,
So I don't really have a clue.

My mum is crazy
And my dad is lazy
My dog is crazy
He makes me dazy.

So it is my family,
They make me jolly,
And I think I'm just like them.

Georgia Lomax-Lane (10)

Fireworks

Fireworks zoom into the sky
Sparkling colours, pretty stars
Rockets shooting into the night
Whizzing out hot fire
Watching fireworks is fun
Be careful with fireworks!

Ben Bradbury (6)

My Lovely Lover

When he jumps to the sky,
He sends a wave of love straight to my heart.
His deep, long ears,
Flap up and down, like the wings of a bird.
His enormous feet, thumping horrendously loud.
I love my Rab so much,
This lover of mine is *hopping mad!*

He's a rabbit!

Arron Andrew Williamson (11)

The City

We are the cars in the city
Scream and roar, scream and roar.

And we are the people that
Walk and talk, walk and talk.

We are the lorries in the city
Zooming by, zooming by.

And we are the people that
Walk and talk, walk and talk.

Conor Sandiford (7)

Naughty Nellie

There was a girl called Naughty Nellie!
Her feet were always hot and smelly!
She's always late because she watches the telly!
Nellie always likes to eat her jelly!
Naughty Nellie! Naughty Nellie!

Saffron Robins (8)

Untitled

The softness of the cats
The wonderful breeze in the trees
The rhythm of the sea
The lovely fish in the sea
The lovely howl of the wind
The soaring of the birds speak to me.

Lowena Mudge (7)

My House

I had a house,
For twenty dares,
So I climbed the
Stairs.

I planted roses
On my door,
But they fell,
On the floor.

The pretty petals
On the nettles
Boiled on the
Kettles.

My fairy godmother
Said,
'Don't bother!'

Shanan Woods (9)

Without You

(Dedicated to Katy O'Hare, my best friend)

Without you I'm like a sun without rays,
A beach without sand or
A clock without hands.

Without you I'm like a class without a teacher,
A nightingale without a voice or
A child with no best friend.

Without you, I'm only half a person.

Katie Pearson (9)

Anger

The feeling of people losing their lives.
The sight of blood when somebody dies.
The sound of bullets flying through the air.
It doesn't seem like anyone actually has a care.

Blood-red, one of the colours of war.
People have been shot, lying on the floor.
Bombs have been dropped, caused a lot of death.
Some of the soldiers hardly get a breath.

Death is black and darkens the sky.
Soldiers marching onward, hoping not to die.
Families running, they are very scared.
Telling their husbands they should not have dared.

Army vs army, loading their guns.
Family after family, losing their sons.

Ryan Turner (10)

Five Little Fishermen

Five little fishermen looking for the oar,
One fell in the water, then there was four.

Four little fishermen going out to sea,
One had a fight and then there was three.

Three little fishermen each saying, *'Boo!'*
One frightened another away, then there was two.

Two little fishermen each had a bun,
They chased the cat away, then there was one.

One little fisherman singing in the sun,
He went to find his friends, then there was none.

Sarah MacLean (7)

My Brother, Harry

My brother Harry
Is bigger than me
But if he is nasty
I can kick him in the knee.

He takes the control
When I am watching TV
Starts flicking the channels
Which really annoys me.

When I get as tall as him
He will be scared out of his skin
And if we get in a fight
I'll chuck him in the bin!

Hayden Cripps (10)

I Need To Go To The Library

I need to go to the library
To read lots and lots of books,
People say I'm going in there
For clumsy librarian looks!

There's lots of grown-up books
And lots of children's too,
There's even a king-size bathroom
With a royalty-styled loo.

There's really nothing here I want
What do you think I should do?
I might just have to switch libraries
Just exactly the same as you!

Ellie Crosby (9)

Mepal

M epal was fun and really nice and marvellous
E xciting, turned scary, but very extraordinary
P laying on the climbing frame and placing out the sand
A rchery was fun, but an aiming game was amazing
L earning about safety and activities, lucky we were

R ock climbing was scary, but was fun, but relieving when you dare
E xciting activity and having lots of fun
S weet at night in the light
I cy and cold, freezing water crystal clear
D ark, warm night and sitting on a bench outside
E ating and drinking, at tea talking
N ight snuggling up tight with our teddy and closing our eyes
T rampolining and flying, bouncing so high
I nspection in the morning and morning greetings
A nd playing with leaders and playing jokes
L aid down in our beds.

Rebecca Stradling (8)

Football Crazy

Football crazy, football mad
Beckham had a hair cut
And Posh went mad.

Football crazy, football mad
Posh brought new glasses
And Beckham was glad.

After they did the limbo dance
Beckham had a phone call to say
He had a match in France.

Ashley Stock (10)

On The Beach

I can hear the seagulls making noises,
I can hear the birds flying past,
I can hear the wind whistling,
I can hear the waves clashing,
I can hear the smashed sandcastles.
I can see the boats and ships sailing,
I can see the beautiful view,
I can see the soggy seaweed on the sand,
I can see the wind blowing the palm trees.
I can feel the ice cream melting in my hand,
I can feel the crab pinching my toe,
I can feel the pebbles by my side,
I can feel the golden sand on my feet,
On the beach!

Meltem Kelmoumin (11)

Autumn

Days are getting colder now
The leaves are different colours
The bears are away to hibernate
Along with all the others

Days are getting darker now
The birds are flying away
The fields are going all misty
While there's colours in the autumn day.

Hannah M Murdoch (10)

The Old Book

When I was young,
Everyone wanted to stare at my pages
As they studied me
My words swam about.

Now, they glance
And fling me in a white wardrobe.

My leaves are brown and weary,
Every day my cover slips away from my spine
It's separated from my pages
Because they're too heavy to grasp.

Who will save me
From my misery?

Selin Özkosar (9)

Life

What is life?
Is life, life
Or is life a quest?
What could or what would
Life bring us ?
Time or new-age?
What is life?
Is life a journey,
Or is life a test?
What is life going to bring us?
Death or birth?

Adeel Ikram (11)

The Three Little Pigs!

Three little pigs built houses one day,
Not a penny did they pay.
The first one made a house of straw,
This was because he was very poor.
The second one built a house of grotty twigs,
These once made lovely figs.
The third one had created a house of bricks,
This one would be easy to fix.
The second day came a big bad wolf,
He said, 'Hi, my name's Gulf!
I want some sugar for my gran,
Caster sugar if you can.'
The pigs thought this was a nasty trick,
Something terrible he would try to nick.
'No!' shouted the three pink pigs
And off they ran to fetch their wigs.
The wolf was cross and gave a puff,
He blew down that straw stuff.
He was mad, so he kicked and kicked,
He knocked down all those mouldy sticks.
Last of all was the house of brick,
This will be very hard to kick.
So he tried to open the front door,
In went the wolf that had broken the law.
He took the caster sugar and a spoon,
It was already past noon.
'I must get back, my gran will worry,'
So the wolf went off in a hurry.
Now the pigs were left with none,
But still, the mean old wolf had gone.

Philippa Kay (10)

Trains In The Future

As the train pulls into the station,
People look for information.
The ticket masters stare and sneer,
The excited customers try not to peer.
People slowly climb onto the train,
One man fell over, he howled in pain.

The alien ticket master pulled a face,
One little girl screamed, she was called Grace.
As the train rode onto the floating tracks,
The people on board put their luggage on racks.
The conductor said, 'Tickets please!'
Then he was attacked by a swarm of bees!

The train strode on, through the air
And then we saw a floating bear.
Suddenly, a rocket jumped in our way,
I wanted a can of coke, but I had to pay.
Then the train landed back on the tracks,
We played cards, I took out the jacks.

As the train glided through the countryside,
I passed some oak trees that were fairly wide.
The birds chirped, sat up in the trees,
Their feathers fluttered gently in the breeze.
The tracks led us through a bright green field,
I could see a remote-controlled church bell being peeled.

At last I've arrived where I'm going to,
I've had fun, how about you?

Jordan Monaghan (10)
Balby Waverley Primary School, Balby

Generation

One morning in the school
I picked up a certain tool
And then I was flying in the air
Going over the fair
Then I fell
Into a well
When I climbed up
I saw a cup.

There were radars on schools
This were the future
There was talking computers
People with jetpacks
Some men with steel walked by
This was unbelievable.

I knew I had to find the tool
To get back to my school
And there it was on the floor
I flew up into the air
I closed my eyes
And I was back.

Adam Dear (9)
Balby Waverley Primary School, Balby

Imagination For A New Generation

In the air there will be
A hover car just for me
No more walking, use a tube
Or a glass box the shape of a cube
Imagination for a new generation.

The trains will go up in the air
You get some food and a comfy chair
Strawberries and cream for a mother
A Gameboy and cake for a brother
Imagination for a new generation.

In every car, they'll be a widescreen
No matter how dirty, your car will still gleam
On the side there will be a big blade
Make the car colour any shade
Imagination for a new generation.

You could buy a hover board
Just made by the big, strong lord
Fire will come out of the end
Ride with one of your favourite friends
Imagination for a new generation.

Rebekka Torshamar (10)
Balby Waverley Primary School, Balby

Imagination For A New Generation

A robot teacher in every class,
A blue, round garden full of grass,
Hover boards to get to school,
Other people will think you're cool,
In the future there will be,
Entertainment for you and me.

Gravity boots to go to space,
There, you'll be in a race,
Fun for children in every room,
So much fun there will be a boom!
In the future there will be,
Bouncy castles for you and me.

All the children will have fun,
Then they will turn very dumb,
Lines for the children when they get done
And always allowed to play in the sun,
In their future there will be,
A funfair for you and me.

Underground school to make the playground bigger,
Underground archaeologists, you may use a digger,
The monkey bars talk and tell,
Then it rings, it rings the bell,
In the future there will be,
Fridays off for you and me!

Megan Wilson (10)
Balby Waverley Primary School, Balby

The Future

In the future there will be,
Fairs in the playground for you and me,
Classrooms will have automatic doors,
Corridors will be filled with silver floors,
We will all have robot teachers
And there will be no more preachers.

Buildings will be flying schools,
In the middle will be big pools,
The children will go and swim in there
While they're eating lovely pears,
Each one will have one big bun
And they will have loads of fun.

Everyone will like my school,
Because it will be really cool,
Pizza for lunch every day,
Except for the day today,
Football for girls is so boring,
So we have to keep on snoring.

The girls like netball,
The boys like football
And a lot of noise
Is normally made by boys,
So we've all decided,
No more football for the boys.
Yes! Yes!

Fiona Kiiza (10)
Balby Waverley Primary School, Balby

In The Future There Will Be . . .

In the future there will be,
Lots of things for you and me,
Fair in the playground and underground schools,
There are lots of things like super pools,
So come on now, join in the fun,
Come on everyone, run, run, run!

My children will be,
Just like me,
They won't get done,
They'll have some fun,
School's sometimes boring,
You hear lots of children snoring.

Children are good,
They play in the mud,
Children play with worms,
In school terms,
The classrooms are brill,
Without a drill.

Computers are ace,
If you work at a pace,
Never work fast,
It's like your past,
Abby gets the best tables,
But writes on all the labels.

Children like to play,
Rather than do their work all day,
Children are scary,
Just like Mary,
Unless they play all day,
In May.

Niki Penn (10)
Balby Waverley Primary School, Balby

The Future

Our school is full of robot teachers,
Camera trackers,
In our school, we have password doors,
We have laminate floors,
In our school we have lots of fun.

Lift-transports, beamed up,
Classes full of kids having their hair done,
Hover boards going up and down,
Outside playing are funny clowns,
In our school we have lots of fun.

Children in their classes doing maths,
Other classes having a laugh,
Children outside playing with their footballs,
People playing in the hall,
In our school we have lots of fun.

Teachers thinking what to do,
While people pretend they're in a canoe,
At dinner time they're allowed out of school,
While people play with their tools,
In our school we have lots of fun.

Fairground in the playground,
While teachers listen to the sound,
Flying schools underground,
While children play with a pound,
In our school we have lots of fun.

In school time if we're good
We should have a concert with lots of fun,
Children running home from school,
Going to play in their pools,
In our school we have lots of fun.

Rikki Fort (11)
Balby Waverley Primary School, Balby

In The Future

In the future I will go teach my school,
When I get there, everybody will be working
So I will shout, *'Cool!'*
Next it would be flying,
So everybody will start sighing,
In the big playground there will be a fair,
But when everybody gets out, they don't care,
There will be automatic doors,
On each one of the floors.

When it's time to eat,
In the dinner hall everyone will meet,
The dinner ladies will be robots
And they'll let you eat lots,
Such as chicken and pies,
Potato wedges and French fries,
After dinner I will just say,
'Come on kids, it's time to play.'

We will play with games,
Before the teacher came,
We can write on the white board,
But before we do, we talk about the Lord,
In the hall we will have pools,
I mean, just how cool, it is my school.

Natalie Ackerman (10)
Balby Waverley Primary School, Balby

The Hi-Tech School

In the future at Waverley School,
Passwords to get in and out of the school
The school is so big
A tube takes us to each lesson.

Laminated flooring in every class,
You don't have to push the door shut anymore,
Just say one word and things will just open
Turn on, turn off, you have no problem anymore.

A tube that takes your register down,
Hover boards to take you to school,
You won't be late now!
No one will skive school
Because school is so cool.

A swimming pool with a roof that closes when it rains,
This school is so good it will be the best in the world,
Air freshener would spray
When someone would belch or trump.

Trampoline, sprint track, swimming pool too,
I bet no one forgets their PE kit now,
A robot cleaner that doesn't lose things,
A football stadium outside,
For Waverley Warriors,
Computers with DVD, video, karaoke and even a TV.

Jamie Veitch (11)
Balby Waverley Primary School, Balby

War In The Next Generation

In the next generation it will be,
Dark and gloomy,
As machines battle for the Earth,
The land is covered in rubble,
For this will be the end of men`.

As screams float into the air,
Running for our lives,
We battle to the bitter end,
For machines are falling
And the age of men grows.

For this will shape the world again,
The planet will not look the same,
Our soldiers are retreating,
There is no hope for us now,
For the machines are moving.

The war is going to end,
There are guns falling,
As are men fighting for their country,
More machines are coming,
For we run towards them,
As sparks fly into the rubble,
Where our men lay,
More machines crashing down.

We see a line of light,
The machines short circuit
And the men drop their guns,
We have won the war!

Craig Sutton (10)
Balby Waverley Primary School, Balby

Time Machine

In the future there will be,
Lots of things for us to see.
Lifts, transporters and hover cars,
Trackers, gravity boots and big radars.

Time machine, time machine, time machine.

Our flying school with a playground fair,
New technology is everywhere,
We've got hover boards and laminate floors,
It's surprising we can fit much more.

Time machine, time machine, time machine.

Real monster that gives you the creeps,
The ones in the closets that always peep!
Lots of snow from a snow machine,
It's the candyfloss man, he's been seen.

Time machine, time machine, time machine.

But just between you and me,
I like the world the way it is, you see.
With working hard and hurting backache,
Lots of writing and things we make.

Time machine, time machine, time machine.

But you get rewarded with a special treat,
Normal teachers that you can't beat.
There's still a life to live, don't waste it,
If you want it to happen, you'll have to make it.

Time machine, time machine, time machine.

Jessica Walsh (10)
Balby Waverley Primary School, Balby

What It Would Look Like In The Future

In the future, the school will put trackers,
So people can't run off,
Virtual football, so you don't have to go outside
So you don't get any cuts or bruises,
A robot teacher who doesn't need food or paying.

Jet packs so you don't need to walk,
Flying schools which fly from country to country
In the blink of an eye,
Hover cars that run on water
And don't affect the ozone layer.

A fairground on the moon and Mars,
Spaceships flying around,
That don't even cost a penny,
Rocket fuel is cheap, as cheap as can be.

Shaun Nazir (10)
Balby Waverley Primary School, Balby

My School In 20 Years

My school in 20 years
Makes all the teachers burst into tears
There are automatic doors,
Ramps all over for hover boards.

Robot teachers take over
This school is only in Dover,
As you see, it's very cool,
It's a well and wicked school.

The teachers have to pay
For them, it's a very boring day,
The teachers have to work,
While the children call them a jerk.

As you can see it's very cool,
It's a well and wicked school.

Joshua Monaghan (9)
Balby Waverley Primary School, Balby

In The Future There Will Be . . .

Fairs in playgrounds are fun ideas,
Automatic doors with glass so clear,
In the future there will be,
Bouncy castles for you and me.

Underground schools attended by tubes,
Classroom doors in shapes of cubes,
In the future there will be,
Pets like dogs and buzzy bees.

Security guards checking on us,
Every day we hear the bees buzz,
In the future there will be,
A camping trip with bacon for tea.

CD players for everyone,
All the old fashioned stuff is all gone,
In the future there will be,
Electric walls with different themes.

Personal organisers for us all,
Sheepskin floors in the dining hall,
In the future there will be,
Robot teachers in the shape of trees.

Flying schools that stop and go,
Gravity boats in rivers that flow,
I'd love to be at school then,
But instead I'll be feeding hens,
Remember the schools will be so great,
You might even have super-small mates.

Dale Storry (10)
Balby Waverley Primary School, Balby

Back To The Future!

In the future there will be
Hover cars for you and me!

In the school there will be
Chocolate pencils for our tea!

In the playground there will be
Fairgrounds on the sea!

In the lunchroom there will be
Transport food for you and me!

In the staffroom there will be
Hover sofas for me to see!

In the toilet there will be
A shower and super drier just for me!

In the cloakroom there will be
Automatic coat hangers for you and me!

In the museum there will be
Technology for me to see!

In the hallway there will be
Weapons to protect us from war to be!

Jordan Hugill (10)
Balby Waverley Primary School, Balby

My Children In My Future

My children in my future,
Thought school rules were cool,
Because they get to go in the pools,
They thinks it's ace,
Because they don't work at a pace
And for school dinners they don't get drool.

They think playtimes are the best,
Because they have a fair and the coolest desk,
My children are the best in class,
No task is too complex or too hard for them.

My future children's teacher,
Looks like a fool,
Because they make her eat school gruel,
In the summer they make her cold,
By putting ice in her clothes.

Now is the time to get revenge on your teacher,
She is like a moving creature
And this is how we will teach her,
When she says, *'You do this!'*
We will all boo and hiss.

At the end of every day,
When all the kids go home to play,
The teacher goes home to pray
For tomorrow to be a better day.

Abby Underwood (9)
Balby Waverley Primary School, Balby

Futurama

The classroom is full of clowns and entertainers,
Outside, the door has got DNA scanners,
Beyond the classroom doors, we have security guards,
To get to every lesson, we ride on hover boards
And for the untidiest classroom, we get the messiest award.

Automatic doors to get into your classroom,
Down in the cellar, to the tomb of doom,
Spaceships flying over the school,
Everybody jumping in the swimming pool,
Most of the people acting cool.

Colourful with rainbow patterns,
The head teacher doesn't care whatever happens,
The teacher is a big, furry monkey,
She acts so very stupidly funky,
Loads to do for me and you,
Hope you come to our wicked school.

Bethany Wrafter (10)
Balby Waverley Primary School, Balby

Untitled

Henry VIII
King Henry VIII was very fierce
And sent his wives all off in tears
Henry loved to eat
But got sore feet
And only lived for a few more years.

Elizabeth I
She was a good queen, Old Queen Bess
But her hair was a bit of a mess
She liked to paint herself white
And wear her clothes tight
And ended the Tudor years with her death.

Mary Leefe (9)
Brooke Hill School, Oakham

Tudor Limericks

The ships in the Armada were great
The sailors got in such a state
As the fire ships were set alight
The Spanish fled just looking at the sight
When the sailors came home, they were late.

Most of the sailors died
Not many survived
That day the queen dressed in black
Sir Francis Drake got the sack
That night, the lords and ladies all cried.

When Queen Elizabeth died
Her people all sighed
Not because they were upset
Because they were not forced to pay their debt
But inside they cried.

Leah Edmonston (10)
Brooke Hill School, Oakham

Henry VIII

King Henry was as fat as a pig
He could have sunk an oil rig
He had six wives
But they lost their lives
Just to make his breakfast big!

Henry couldn't bear his life
He really wanted another wife
For the final one, Katherine Parr,
She must survive without a fear,
She mustn't let him near the knife.

Charlie Dearden (10)
Brooke Hill School, Oakham

Henry's Witches

There was a fat English king,
Who loved to dance and sing,
He had many wives,
So these are their lives,
When married to the fat English king!

Poor Catherine of Aragon first,
Her marriage wasn't the worst,
But the girl was boring,
So Henry sent her touring
And then her bubble was burst!

Anne Boleyn was a prettier girl,
In her gorgeous clothes she did twirl,
But she had a sharp mouth
And boyfriends in the south,
So Henry made the death note unfurl!

Good old Jane Seymour was next,
She liked to read play's text,
She was bright, like the sun
And gave Henry a son,
But died and it made Henry vexed!

Anne of Cleves, the Flanders mare,
Gave old King Henry a scare,
She thought she was pretty,
Which was a pity,
For she looked like a cow or a bear!

Catherine Howard was a beautiful being,
Henry was stunned at what he was seeing,
But she loved another boy
And Henry was just her toy,
So to death he sent her fleeing!

The last was Katherine Parr,
But the marriage never went far,
When they became good friends,
Henry met his end
And Katherine became a star!

Daisy Crump (10)
Brooke Hill School, Oakham

Tudor Times

Edward VI
Young Edward VI was fed arsenic
He then lay in his bed, very sick,
For six years Eddie reigned
His courtiers were blamed,
But his sister went even more quick.

Mary I
Our old Mary Tudor became the first
She may have been the worst,
She burnt enemies at the stake
This was a real mistake,
Because in the end, she burst.

Spanish Armada
The Armada was spotted from the coast
All the Spanish could do was boast,
The English made fire ships,
The fire burnt to the mast's tips,
The Spanish ships were burnt to toast.

The Spanish didn't see the Duke of Parma
The Spanish lost most of their armour
They never reached England
They didn't see any sand
And the sea never got calmer.

Martha Clewlow (9)
Brooke Hill School, Oakham

Tudor Limericks

Poor little Ed
Lay down in his bed
He started to cry
Because he knew he would die
And in the morning
Poor little Ed
Was dead.

The Tudors went on to Mary
The Tudors became more scary
The Tudors went on
Until they were done
That was the end of Mary.

Elizabeth came to the throne
She looked like she was only bone
Lizzie was so tall
Which made Henry look small
That was the end of the Tudors.

Georgina Baker (10)
Brooke Hill School, Oakham

Untitled

Anne was a six-fingered dame
Who was always the one to blame
She haunts her London tower
And has deadly ghost powers
And has never been quite the same.

Catherine of Aragon was Henry's first wife
He was having the time of his life
The marriage had just begun
When Catherine could not give him a son
So he decided to end her life.

Holli Munford (10)
Brooke Hill School, Oakham

Queen Elizabeth

A harsh lived life had Queen Lizzie
All those beacons must make a woman dizzy
The Spanish Armada and all
When we won, she must have had a ball
I'm sure old Lizzie was very busy.

All those sailors at sea
Fighting for our country
All those cannon balls
The men who made those calls
And Lizzie sat down and had tea.

It's coming to the end of her reign
She doesn't want to die in pain
Now it's all over
She slept like a clover
Never to awake again.

Jamie Williamson (11)
Brooke Hill School, Oakham

Untitled

Henry VIII was as big as a ship
His clothes, all they did were rip
His buttons strained
His weight gained
Then *crack* went his hip.

Henry VIII was so great
He ruled so very late
He had a lot of brain
He gave people the cane.

Hannah Elthorpe (9)
Brooke Hill School, Oakham

Tudor Limericks

Poor old Anne of Cleves
Henry hid under his sleeves
He ran away and hid
Just like a big kid
Now all he eats is peas.

Good old King Ed
Didn't like going to bed
He was king at nine
He whined all the time
Now he's not so steady.

Amy Carter (10)
Brooke Hill School, Oakham

Untitled

Lady Jane Grey
Poor Lady Jane Grey
Only reigned for about a day
Until Mary the first
Came in a burst
Then Jane was covered in hay.

Mary I
Mary Tudor loved to burn
That made the Protestants learn
Mary was married to the King of Spain
Who was a real pain
I don't think anybody liked her turn.

Aaron Roy (9)
Brooke Hill School, Oakham

Henry VIII

King Henry was as fat as a pig
And still was growing too big
He broke his posh bed
And fell on his head
And had to buy a new wig.

King Edward was the king to become
He was Henry's first son
The throne was pink
He didn't like the sink
And didn't think this would be much fun.

Emily Bailey (11)
Brooke Hill School, Oakham

Tudor Times

There was a young lady in Tudor times
Who loved to tell rhymes
She said one day
'Will the rain go away
Because my washing's out on the line.'

There was a young man in Tudor times
Who loved to commit awful crimes
He said one day
'Will my wife go away
So I can wed for the sixth time!'

Emma Williams (10)
Brooke Hill School, Oakham

Worms

Worms
live
underground:
deep
under
the
surface;
helping
a
farmer's
crops.

Asher Oliver (7)
Chapel Primary School, Chapel-en-le-Frith

Raindrops

Raindrops, *pitter-patter,*
Dropping from the sky.
They fall all around the world.
They make my hair wet
And make my coat all soaked.
Sometimes they get heavier and heavier.
It makes a noise on my window.
It makes a noise on my door.
All they do is make puddles
For us to splash in.

Rebecca Green (7)
Chapel Primary School, Chapel-en-le-Frith

Drip Drop

Falling, falling, *splash!*
Into the river,
Then to the sea.

Drip-drop.
Down from the sky,
Pitter-patter
On the roof.

Frozen, it forms snow.
Coats on everybody!
The hoods of our coats
Will stop our heads getting wet.

Heavy rain and showers,
Drizzle and sleet.
The rain soaks everybody.

Rain shaped like peas and circles,
With the bottom chopped off.

Martyn Bonham (7)
Chapel Primary School, Chapel-en-le-Frith

Leaves

Leaves are crispy.
Some are big,
Some are small,
Some are red,
Some are brown,
Some are yellow,
That fall off the tree.
Some leaves have holes in them.
Some don't.
Leaves crunch.

Adam Barnes (7)
Chapel Primary School, Chapel-en-le-Frith

Worm

Fat, juicy, lovely worm
A bird is watching him with hawk eyes
Worm, worm, can he escape?
It looks like the bird will be having him
In a big, juicy cake
The bird is pulling him out
With a big, big heave!
He's been here since
Christmas Eve!

Benjamin Hall (7)
Chapel Primary School, Chapel-en-le-Frith

Leaves

Brown, orange, red and yellow.
Holly leaves falling off the trees.
Crispy, crackly and crunchy leaves.
Rip, rip, rip.
Big, small and medium leaves
And any shape.

Rebecca Ryan (7)
Chapel Primary School, Chapel-en-le-Frith

Ice Cream

I love ice creams
I want one now
I really like a lovely ice cream
They are so lovely
I want one now
Cos they are very sloppy
And very sticky and melty
God made ice cream.

Thomas Anderson (7)
Chapel Primary School, Chapel-en-le-Frith

Ice Cream

Sloppy, icy, cold.
Sloppy, icy, cold.

Icy and cold
My ice cream has melted.
It was like a house
And tastes nice
I got another one.

Sloppy, icy, cold.
Sloppy, icy, cold.

Fiona Biggin (7)
Chapel Primary School, Chapel-en-le-Frith

Children

Some children come fast.
Children come last.
Children are slow.
Children speed.
Children meet in a running race.
Children just carry on.
Children cheat.
Children think they're going.
Children win.
Children lose.

George Buxton
Chapel Primary School, Chapel-en-le-Frith

The Snail

The swirling shell,
Those slimy tracks,
Always chasing interesting facts.

He's ever so slow,
His beady eyes, looking around,
He'll stick on your hand, I've found,
A mini slug,
A mobile home.

Bethanie Williamson (10)
Chapel Primary School, Chapel-en-le-Frith

Uniform

Grey trousers, navy jumper
And my shiny black shoes.
White shirt and tie,
The uniform I didn't choose.
Smart we look
So into school
I like my uniform, it looks so cool.

Cian Kavanagh (8)
Christ The King Catholic Junior School, Coundon

Homework

School work can be fun
But homework must be done,
It sometimes seems a chore
And homework is a bore,
But mostly it is fun
When all the homework's done
Then we can play with friends
Until the evening ends.

Danielle Friel (8)
Christ The King Catholic Junior School, Coundon

Indoor Play

The bell starts to ring,
'Yippee!' the children sing.
Oh no, what a pain,
It's pouring down with rain.
Never mind the weather,
We'll all play together.
Who cares about the sun,
Indoor playtime's fun.

Natasha Rollason (8)
Christ The King Catholic Junior School, Coundon

School Uniform

The trousers I wear are grey
The same as the start of the day
The shirt I wear is white
When the sun shines it looks extra bright.

Black is the colour of my shoes
My jumper and tie are two blues
My uniform looks rather smart
And when I am dressed I look the part.

Sean Cavigan (8)
Christ The King Catholic Junior School, Coundon

Day At School

Walking in the morning
On my way to school
Jumper, hat, scarf and gloves
Makes me feel a fool.

School bag on my back
Really weighs me down
Other children laugh and play
But all I do is frown.

Emily Holland (8)
Christ The King Catholic Junior School, Coundon

School Dinners

I love school dinners
I think they're yum
I could gobble them up
Until they fill my tum.
I could eat that much
That my shirt wouldn't fit
But I must be careful
In case my trousers split.
So I watch my diet
And eat with care
I stay fit and healthy
Which I think is fair.

Christie O'Toole (8)
Christ The King Catholic Junior School, Coundon

Break Time

Monday's bell rings out loud,
We laugh as we run to the crowd.
Tuesday's bell rings out loud,
We're inside, look at those clouds.
Wednesday's bell rings out loud,
Girls skip on ropes, boys run around.
Thursday's bell rings out loud
We pray in our garden, the birds tweet around.
Friday's bell rings out loud,
I'm smiling because the weekend has come round.

Eleanor McKeown (8)
Christ The King Catholic Junior School, Coundon

Homework Poem!

Homework can be hard
But also very good.
Giving me more knowledge
So it can be understood.
Lots of many hours
Sitting at the table.
Reading, writing and thinking
Doing my times tables.
Oh, so very tired now
Can't think of anymore questions
In my tiny head.
Put my things away
I'm off to my bed.

Elissa Sheehan (8)
Christ The King Catholic Junior School, Coundon

School Dinners

I'm sitting eating my peas and carrots
While everyone chatters like squawking parrots.
Smooth, creamy custard and apple pie
Not my favourite, don't really know why.
Cherry-topped biscuit, that's the best
Better make sure I get there before the rest.
Now I really want to go out and play
So it's time to eat up and clear away.

James Mohan (8)
Christ The King Catholic Junior School, Coundon

Literacy Homework

I was given some homework,
I hadn't a clue,
What I was writing,
Or what I should do.
A poem on a school theme,
Or maybe the football team,
Oh, the decision is far too hard,
I'd much rather go out and play in the yard!
Miss Caley said, 'Work and pay attention.'
But if I don't finish, I might get a detention!

Sarah Molloy (8)
Christ The King Catholic Junior School, Coundon

Homework

There was a young lady called Lydia Black,
Who brought her homework home in a sack.
Then emptied the contents over the kitchen table,
To prove that she was willing and able.
To do her homework in time and style,
Therefore, getting it back in a nice, neat pile.
The aim was to get a good mark,
So she could rest and play at the park.
So proving that Lydia Black was willing and able,
To sit and do her homework at the kitchen table.

Lydia Black (8)
Christ The King Catholic Junior School, Coundon

School Team

Hooray, hooray, it's Thursday
My favourite day of the week.
It's 3.45 and football time
We better get to our feet.
We run around no matter
What we won't be seen as weak.
We love the game and want to win
And with this training we are at our peak.

Christopher Kelly (8)
Christ The King Catholic Junior School, Coundon

Time To Play

Playground, playground, we play on it.
Playground, playground, we sit on it.
Goodness, goodness, that will be sound.
Goodness, goodness, that will be found.
Playing, playing, that's what we do.
Playing, playing, do you want to?
Running, running, I am high speed.
Running, running, I am in the lead.

Caitlin Reidy (8)
Christ The King Catholic Junior School, Coundon

Going To School

I love going to school
It's really rather cool.

Our uniform is neat
We look smart from our heads to our feet.

Mum says, 'It's far,'
So we go in the car.

But going to school is a treat.

Charlotte Evatt (8)
Christ The King Catholic Junior School, Coundon

Grandma Of The Night

The night is like my grandma
It feels lovely and warm.

It takes my hand
She understands me
The night tiptoes all around
When children are going to sleep.

Night lives with the sparkling stars
Gently in my dreams.

When I close my eyes
I can smell beautiful roses
Floating in the breeze
I can feel the night
Cuddling me when I am drifting off to sleep.

I look at her one last time
Then she disappears.

Laoura Parginou (11)
Coppull Parish Church School, Coppull

The Phantom's Back

I met, at eve, the cruel and nasty phantom.
The phantom that will take you away
When you fall asleep.

When you're on your own, you should be terrified,
But don't fall asleep because he will grab you.

The phantom creeps and roams down the streets.

You will know if you see him
Because he has a dark green face
And red flashing eyes, big, sharp teeth.

If I was you, I wouldn't go near his haunted house
Or he will grab you and kill you.

Laura Wareing (10)
Coppull Parish Church School, Coppull

My Demon Dream

I met a demon of sleep
His flaming eyes shining under his hood
His creepy black claws holding his sharp axe
Swish, slash, a telephone post falls down.

He roams around his deadly lair
Planning his next attack
He creeps up to a house
Waits until you're in a deep sleep
He sneaks up to you
And whips you on his back.

He screams and he screams
But the boy cannot be heard
The demon ends his life
With a hot death.

But the boy's coming back
Out of the lair, back to life
The demon's melting in the ground
I'll be back!' he shouts.
'Muhuhahaha!'

Cameron Sharratt
Coppull Parish Church School, Coppull

Hate And Love

Hate is a bad thing
Love is good
People should never hate
But love they should.

Yesterday I hated someone
And then I thought of love
I must never hate
And neither should you.

Liam Mutch (10)
Coppull Parish Church School, Coppull

Diamond Night

Night is a gentle lady,
Every night she swiftly moves,
Through the streets, listening,
Whenever a soul is awake,
She silently glides away.

Her hair is as gold as gold can be,
It glistens in the moonlight,
Her eyes are blue and bright,
They shine in the night,
Her mouth sparkles,
Bright and pink.

As she walks,
Her white, silky dress
Follows her repeatedly,
As she strolls
She gently picks out which star will shine
The brightest all through the night.

Once the night is over
She glides up to her home in the sky
And silently watches and waits,
For the sun to set
And for the moon to rise,
Not knowing what to expect for the awaiting night.

Rianne Holme (11)
Coppull Parish Church School, Coppull

I Met Him At Midnight

I met him at midnight,
His bloodthirsty fangs,
His ten foot long luminous tongue
And his long, hollow, everlasting mouth,
I met him at midnight.

Night creeps up on little children
Frightening them and scaring them,
He makes you feel lonely,
You feel your inside's turning inside out,
You sweat, you toss and turn,
But all you can hear is the wind through your hair
It's quiet, too quiet.

Night is like a raging sea,
Freezing cold and not refreshing,
Slithering through cracks in the doors
And through the walls and up the floors,
He is a horrible thing, is night
He is a raging sea.

He can swallow you up into darkness,
So never go out at night when you are alone,
In the day he hides behind people,
They think it's just a shadow,
But we know otherwise, don't we?

Adam Bennett (10)
Coppull Parish Church School, Coppull

The Sun Sucker

I met a vampire; a vampire of the night
He always sucks the sun away
So it is dark every day
And every step I take, he follows me.

His face is wrinkled every day
His body is as pale as a ghost's
He always swishes into the darkness
So nobody can see him.

He loses all of his power
So the sun comes up
And he slowly fades away
He will return and do the same.

Shaun Greenhalgh (11)
Coppull Parish Church School, Coppull

I Met At Twelve

I met at twelve
The ghost of night
As he loomed down the streets.
His misty, murky face showing
A blurry smile.
His hair wavy,
His eyes glint
And clothes ripped and torn.

He comes and goes
From head to head
Making you tired and sleepy
And there he goes
The ghost of night
Back to his lair.

Alex Winward (10)
Coppull Parish Church School, Coppull

The Creeper

Night is the king of sleep
His old and wrinkled face
As he creeps through the streets
And looms above your roof.

His old and lonely figure
Watches you wherever you are
He can see you, even if you're in bed
He'll be watching and waiting for his next victim.

Then he creeps into your house
Then he crawls up the stairs
And opens the bedroom door
Then sneaks up to the bed
And snatches the child
And goes back to his dark lair.

The child screams, but no one hears him
As he is taken to the lair of the night
Then he slays the child
Then the night sleeps and waits for tomorrow night.

Jonathon South (10)
Coppull Parish Church School, Coppull

The Executioner

Night is a shadowy character
He creeps up on people
People get the shivers
People think he is a shadow
But it is night.

He wears a dark, black gown
And has red, fiery eyes
And a hood that covers his forehead
And he hovers along the ground.

Joe David Squires (10)
Coppull Parish Church School, Coppull

Phantom Of The Night

The night is a phantom
As mean as can be
He roams around the streets at night
His footsteps on the cobblestones
Thundering like a drum
With bloodshot eyes
And a face as black as black
He finds his victims wisely.

When you're asleep
He's watching you
The phantom of the night
He's stirring up your dreams
You'll jump and leap and yelp!
When you see his monstrous face.

When you hear him groan and gasp
And just as soon as he had come
The sun rose and he had gone.

Gemma Coulthard (10)
Coppull Parish Church School, Coppull

Night

Night is a warm, calm and soft nan.
She makes me feel nice, warm and comfy.
Her face looks old and wrinkled.
Her eyes are flaming like fire.
Her mouth is shaped like a love heart.
Her hair is as curly as a poodle's.
Her clothes are made of fluffy wool.
She moves very slowly and calmly.
When she speaks, her voice is croaky like a witch's.
She lives in a cottage with me.
Night is kind to me.

Jean Penney (10)
Coppull Parish Church School, Coppull

I Met At Eve

Night is caring and loving like my father
He makes me feel like am the happiest boy in the world
Night's face looks like a friendly, pale white face
His eyes are shiny-blue beautiful eyes.

Night's mouth has shiny gold lips
And sparkling white teeth
His hair is nice, black hair, as black as a piece of coal
Night wears a long, white cloak, as white as a big, white cloud
When night moves, all you can hear
Are his feet trembling in the clouds.

When night speaks, it's like you have just heard God speaking
He lives in a big castle with a monumental door
And a flying car in the garage.

Night loves me.

Michael Ian Thomas (10)
Coppull Parish Church School, Coppull

Night Is Nice To Me

Night is a nice, calm place
He makes me feel safe and secure
His face looks soft and smooth
His eyes are as black as coal and as big as saucers
He has a mouth that smiles brightly
And teeth that dazzle in the dark night
His hair is grey with age
Hanging loosely under his kingly crown
He wears a red, silken cloak, trimmed with wool
He moves slowly in the night, like a serpent slithering away
When he speaks, his voice is soft and quiet
He lives behind the sun, with the moon and the stars
Night is nice to me.

Michael Tasker (11)
Coppull Parish Church School, Coppull

Night Watch

I met at eve, the princess of sleep
With her silky, warm glow
She stumbles through the streets at night
And blows dreams through the window.

The kind and helpful princess
Watches over you at night
She sits on her throne in the sky
And watches over you at night.

But when you're having the time of your life
Everything has to end
Everything goes quiet
You've woken up again.

Abbigail Meegan (10)
Coppull Parish Church School, Coppull

Night

Night is a caring grandma
She makes me feel like I'm very pretty
Her face looks old and wrinkly
Her eyes are the colour of baby-blue
Her mouth is shaped like a love heart when she kisses me
Her hair is as long as a horse's tail and very blonde
Her clothes are made of silk
She moves very slowly and calmly
She speaks in an old, croaky voice
She lives in a house with her puppies and kittens
Night is kind to me
Is night kind to you?

Katie McNamara (11)
Coppull Parish Church School, Coppull

The Night That Makes You Smile

Night is a beautiful prince
He is always caring
And helps you think of lovely thoughts.

His face is smooth
And is a gentle face
He's kind and he always smiles at you
And thinks of you.

His eyes are black and fiery
But they gloom at you and glisten at you
They shine and shock you
He always has a cheery smile on his face
And laughs at you too.

His hair is straight, lovely and thick
He wears his armour, silver and shiny
So he looks smart.

He goes strolling through the streets
Wondering what to do
He speaks deeply and loud
He always speaks to himself.

He lives in a castle
With his maids
And his friends.

Night comforts me.

Alice Bury (10)
Coppull Parish Church School, Coppull

The Night That Looms Upon You!

I met a prince, the prince of night
He has a grey and misty face
He roams through the streets at night
Creeps around every corner.
His hair is black, as black as night
He smiles a wide and greedy smile
His eyes flash like traffic lights
Around the streets so dark.

During the day he hides away in his house
Chats to phantoms that come through his walls
And sleeps till night comes around
Sometimes he wanders around the dungeon of death
And stares at the blood on the floor.
Night after night he roams around every corner
Haunting people who walk by
Glaring at people through windows
And wishing that they'd see him and cry.

Then he sees a person
He tackles, tugs and pulls him
Then he drags his victim
To the dungeon of death.
He leaves you hanging from the wall
Then cackles loudly
As you struggle to get free.

You ask yourself
Does he really enjoy torturing me?
How could he be so cruel?
Then, all of a sudden, you wake up
And look around your bedroom
Everything is normal again
Or is it?

Rebecca Bradley (10)
Coppull Parish Church School, Coppull

The Misty Devil

He comes out at night and wakes with a big roar
And he goes out to make trouble.
He stands on top of the mist and lurks around
Trying to find a boy to kill.
He goes into his misty house and runs to a drawer
And gets the knife of doom!
He walks out and leaps off the misty sky.

He hits the floor and his misty feet run to a fence
And jumps on the fence
And watches a house to see if the family has a boy or a girl
But if they do not have a boy or girl
He will watch for a car and get a juicy child.

He will get his sharp teeth out
And will pull his hood up
And his eyes will start flaming when he sees a child
But when the car goes past, he roars.

He jumps onto the car
Then rips the children out
And then pulls them up to the sky and then . . .
Lets them go, so they hit the floor and die.
But if you are still alive
He will chase you through the street
And he will start walking
And his eyes will glow at you
It will stop you running
And you will not be seen again.

He wears a dark, black hoodie
And dark green pants
And he has no feet, so he hovers
He will roar all night, if he does not find a child
He will turn into an animal
So a child will follow.

Nathan Bennett (10)
Coppull Parish Church School, Coppull

Love Can Be Sensitive

One time, I met the God of Love,
Sweet and kind and gentle in your arms.
His coloured hair sways in the wind
Whilst he thinks of his victory.
What can he stop, except from the hatred . . . ?

People might not like seeing the love
Whereas some do.
The appearance might be deceiving
But the love can be inside,
He would jump around trying to stop these awful wars
But sometimes he fails his duty!

He tries to kill the pain,
But people just want more . . .
The time spent being free in the peaceful wind
And then you stumble upon the God of Love
And your life goes on to the end of happiness.

Where could this love be hiding?
Is it true he's ran away in misery
Or has he just found his rightful place of love?
Where his duty will carry on . . .

With this rumble and terror, will he be pleased . . . ?
Where he lingers in the doorway,
Hoping for this horror to end.
He stops around his story tale
Trapped inside himself for hours.

Only if this would turn out happy,
Where people could share their love
Instead of killing its soul!
Where he hears the crushing of his heart
And hopes for this nightmare to end.

When he defeats the enemy of his hatred
And creates the circle of love together again,
The war will end with many people injured
With their souls broken . . .
He would heal these wounds with his loving happiness
To help a suffering friend.

He wanders the night-time streets
Back to the peaceful way it should be
And watches people sleep,
Love can be sensitive.

Andy Holme (11)
Coppull Parish Church School, Coppull

The Fairy Of The Night

Night is a glowing, beautiful fairy,
She makes me feel safe and warm,
She wouldn't let anyone harm me
And always keeps an eye on me,
She makes me have sweet dreams,
That I can never forget about,
She has pink cheeks that never fade away.

Her eyes are as black as blackcurrants,
Her teeth are as white as pearls in a jewellery box,
Her hair is blonde,
Her curls dangle down her back,
Her dress has pink jewels all over
And trails on the floor.

When the wind blows
And she blinks
It's like the stars twinkling
She lies with the stars till she falls asleep,
Falls asleep,
When it rains, she will cover me up
With her big, fluffy wings
She glides up past the big, bright sun,
Then she waits for the moon to rise
And the stars to come out and twinkle.

Claudia Westhead (10)
Coppull Parish Church School, Coppull

A Helpful Night

I met at eve
The policeman of the night
With a skip in his step
And a jolly whistle.

With big, black, polished shoes
And an enormous black hat
As black as a panther's black fur
And a black uniform
With a shining badge
Glistening in the sky.

Watching all the houses
It was peaceful
All you could hear
Was the whistle
Of the wind.

A misty house at the top of a hill
He ran up to the house
I ran after him
He caught the burglar
And soon he was back in the village
Watching the people sleep.

Soon he fades away
It's day and now we can play
And go to school.

Emily Borrowdale (10)
Coppull Parish Church School, Coppull

Happiness Is . . .

Happiness is seeing my little, fluffy cat
Happiness is hearing my mum shouting for me
Happiness is smelling my mum's lovely hot dogs
Happiness is tasting my favourite fish and chips
Happiness is touching my cute little brother's soft skin.

Poppy Jane Bellerby (8)
Crossflatts Primary School, Crossflatts

The Storm

The storm
Scatters through the woods
Flashes as quick as a leopard runs
Zooms past trees, flickering.

The storm
Crashes as it crackles by
Hooting louder than an owl
Shrieks like a giant's foot hitting the ground.

Bethanie Dunning (9)
Crossflatts Primary School, Crossflatts

On The 5th Of November

Lots of fireworks in the sky,
Look at all the people, oh my, oh my,
See the bonfire in the park,
'Oh look, it's already dark,'
Hot dogs being eaten in a dash,
'Wow! That was a big flash!'
People laughing and talking,
Look at all the people gawking.

Laura Foy (8)
Crossflatts Primary School, Crossflatts

Bonfire Night

Zooming rocket quickly,
Sugary chocolate apples sweetly . . .
Swirling Catherine wheels loudly!
Smoky fire flaming,
Steaming smoke flying,
Sizzling sparklers swirling,
Black bonfire lollies yummy,
Horrible bonfire sweets yucky.

Benjamin Whitfield (8)
Crossflatts Primary School, Crossflatts

Sounds

The happiest sound in the world
Must be babies chuckling
When they are playing with their toys.

The spookiest sound in the world
Must be a ghost singing on a stage
In the most haunted castle in the world.

The saddest sound in the world
Must be a little girl
Being bullied by an older boy.

The most dangerous sound in the world
Must be a gun
Shot in the air.

The quickest sound in the world
Must be the sound of a fast racing car
Zooming down the road.

Ellie Morris (7)
Crossflatts Primary School, Crossflatts

Lauren's Pets

Ten horses sleeping under the bed.
Nine slugs ugly and sweet.
Eight snails slithering on the bed.
Seven donkeys sitting on the bed.
Six birds sitting on my knee.
Five leopards climbing the tree.
Four frogs swimming in the pond.
Three monkeys swinging in the tree.
Two cats running round and round.
One snake slithering up and down.

Lauren Corby (8)
Crossflatts Primary School, Crossflatts

Mum Won't Let Me Keep A Rabbit

Mum won't let me keep a viper
She won't let me keep a bat
She won't let me keep a bull
Or even a cat with a top hat.

She won't let me keep a spider
She won't let me keep a dog
She won't let me keep a rattlesnake
Or even a frog in a bog.

I can't keep a deer
Or an ant in the house
I can't keep a cat
A lizard or a mouse.

Elliott Bedford (8)
Crossflatts Primary School, Crossflatts

Happiness Is . . .

Happiness is eating ice cream
Happiness is doing PE
Happiness is looking after my brother
Happiness is eating chocolate Maltesers
Happiness is a nice teacher
Happiness is a good friend
Happiness is a helicopter
Happiness are my rabbits
Happiness is swimming
Happiness is . . .

Lauren Calvert (8)
Crossflatts Primary School, Crossflatts

Untitled

There was an old lady
Whose kitchen was bare
So she called for the cat
Saying, 'Time for some air!'

She sent him to buy her
A slice of ham
But he rushed back
With his cousin Sam.

She sent him to buy her
A packet of cheese
But he came back
With three dozen trees.

She sent him to buy her
A loaf of bread
But he ran back
With a cat's head.

Lauren John (7)
Crossflatts Primary School, Crossflatts

Bonfire Night

Spitting sparklers swirling,
Crunchy mushy peas, lovely,
Grey smoke smells,
Bright fire sizzling,
Big Catherine wheels, loud,
Hot pie, cool . . .
Big rocket, *wow!*
Sugar toffee apples, yum.

Hollie Whitford (8)
Crossflatts Primary School, Crossflatts

The Sounds Around Me

The spookiest sound in the world
Is the door creaking very slowly.

The happiest sound in the world
Is when my mum says she loves me.

The noisiest sound in the world
Must be when my mum shouts.

The quietest sound in the world
Is when my dog walks carefully.

Aaron Lee Tscherniga (7)
Crossflatts Primary School, Crossflatts

Animal

The cheetah
Hunts along the grass
Sprints to catch animals
Stalks under branches
And pounces on zebras.

The cheetah
Purrs when it is hungry
Roars at enemies
Pants after a fight
And yawns after a long day.

Sam Bone (7)
Crossflatts Primary School, Crossflatts

There Was An Old Lady

There was an old lady
Whose kitchen was bare
So she called for the cat
Saying, 'Time for some air!'

She sent him to buy her
A loaf of bread
But the cat appeared back
With 17 heads,

She sent him to buy her
A nice cup of tea
But the cat hurried back
With some water from the sea.

She sent him to buy her
A little bit of ham
But the cat scampered back
With a boy called Sam.

She sent him to buy her
A tin of sweetcorn
But the cat ran back
With a rhino's horn.

The fridge was soon jammed
And so was the shelf
So he sent for a pizza
And ate it himself.

Hannah Foy (8)
Crossflatts Primary School, Crossflatts

Bonfire Night

Brown hot dog yum
Crunchy flapjack delicious
Colourful fireworks fantastic
Spinning sparklers cool
Green apples tasty
Rustling fire great
Whistling smoke stinky
Crispy pie lovely
Chocolate doughnut yummy.

Lauren Benson (7)
Crossflatts Primary School, Crossflatts

Flowers

I like the smell of . . .
Colourful things,
Bright things,
Outstanding things,
Red things,
Yellow things,
Small things,
Pretty things,
Wonderful things.
I like the smell of flowers.

Bekki Carragher (10)
Eastcroft Park CP School, Knowsley

Untitled

I like the feel of . . .
Cuddly stuff,
Soft stuff,
Glass-eyed stuff,
Hairy stuff,
Fluffy stuff,
Warm stuff,
Brown stuff,
Furry stuff.
I like the feel of teddy bears.

Carl Evans (11)
Eastcroft Park CP School, Knowsley

My Mum And Dad

I love my mum and dad,
They really are quite mad!
My mum and dad are truly the best,
They never stop to have a rest!
I always see them with a smile,
They are the best parents by a mile!

Kellie Carragher (9)
Eastcroft Park CP School, Knowsley

Different Girls' Names

There are lots of different girls in my school
And some of their names are really cool.
Sarah, Jenny
Jessica and Penny
And Chloe who hangs around with Zoe
Lauren, Emma
Jane and Gemma
Devon, Brendy
Kelly and Wendy
A very funny girl called Zara,
A very groovy girl called Tara.
There are lots of girls who are sunny.
There are lots of girls who are funny.

Helen Greaves (9)
East Stanley School, East Stanley

My Favourite PC Games

Age of Empires, the Conqueror is cool.
I like The Sims when you go in the pool.
Theme Park World when you make the park,
I can't forget Noah's Ark.
And Call For Duty,
Prince of Persia is a beauty.
Lego Races
Funny Faces
Jurassic Park is a shoot-'em-up.
Underworld is a game that makes you throw up in a cup.

Nathan Brown (9)
East Stanley School, East Stanley

Zigger-Wigger

Along the orchard of the apple trees
Comes the awful smell of cheese
The people say here comes the Zigger-Wigger on his way
You can hear him coming, because the sound of his feet is *plod, plod*
And then you can hear people sobbing, *sob, sob*
But it's even worse when he hears the aeroplanes
And then starts to go badly insane
His eyes go fiery-red
That's when everyone hides in their beds
He roars and he pours out with tears
Everyone hears.

Alice Fletcher (8)
Eton Wick CE First School, Eton Wick

The Garden

I walked in my garden and what did I see?
A shiny red apple sitting on a branch, looking at me.
The sun shone bright in the sky
The leaves in the trees wiggling up high.
Flowers bright with lots of colours
Creatures crawling in and out of burrows.
The fresh grass was as green as can be
The swimming pool made you think of the sea.

My garden is the best in the world.

Georgia McGlasson (7)
Eton Wick CE First School, Eton Wick

Animals

The fire from a dragon may destroy a village
The roar of a lion may hurt your ears
The long neck of a giraffe may make you think you're a mouse
And the horn of a rhino may make you terrified.

Stanley Clifford (7)
Eton Wick CE First School, Eton Wick

An Imaginary Room

Silky, pink curtains hiding the sunlight
A wooden, brown door, keeping people out
The hard, pink walls to keep the room safe
The huge blue hairband that holds up a ponytail
The fluffy pink rug making your feet relax
A little red poppy for Remembrance Day
A magical, red basket holding all my books
The mysterious multicoloured book helping me to learn
The metal, blue pencil case holding all my stationery pieces.

Eleanor O'Donnell (8)
Eton Wick CE First School, Eton Wick

An Extraordinary Room

A stiff, white door not letting people in,
Colourful, pink walls making my room mysterious,
Multicoloured books giving us imagination,
Hairy, purple rug tickling you when you walk,
Lively, blue lampshade helping you to see in the dark,
Magical, brown desk doing your homework for you,
Puffy, gold pillowcases giving you a good night's sleep,
Annoying, silver wardrobe hiding all your clothes,
Extremely sticky, violet wall stickers making your room feel magical.

Hannah Davies (7)
Eton Wick CE First School, Eton Wick

Roses Are Red, Violets Are Blue

Roses are red, violets are blue.
The whole world is green and blue.
Roses are red, violets are blue.
The whole sun is hot and huge.
Roses are red, violets are blue.
The stars are sparkly and beautiful.

Charlotte Bone (7)
Eton Wick CE First School, Eton Wick

Baby

My auntie's got a bump
And I know what it is going to be.
Let me tell you what it is
It's gonna be a beautiful baby.
It is sure to bring her happiness
It is sure to bring her joy.
I am sure it will bring her all these things
Either a girl or a boy.
It's coming up to Christmas
So let us get out our tree.
The best present I could ever have
Is a beautiful baby!

Bethany Taylor (8)
Eton Wick CE First School, Eton Wick

The Garden

What's in my garden . . . ?
A bird singing in a tree,
The sun high in the sky,
Some people playing football in the sun,
Some apples on a high tree,
A cat on the roof of my house,
A tree leaning to one side,
A girl skipping all day long,
Some lovely, green grass,
My mum gardening.

Daniel George Morgan (8)
Eton Wick CE First School, Eton Wick

Monsters In My Bedroom

Monsters in my bedroom
Running all around
On Monday I saw a Yeti's shadow
On Tuesday I saw a three-headed scorpion leading a troop
On Wednesday I saw a UFO
On Thursday I saw a skeleton leading an army
On Friday I saw a tarantula with ten legs
On Saturday I saw a dead person in a pirate's hands
On Sunday I saw a vampire in my bed.

Jake Church (7)
Eton Wick CE First School, Eton Wick

Hallowe'en

H allowe'en is great
A ltogether scary
L ots of fun
L aughing all the way
O h, so very frightening
W alking along trick or treating
E ee, I love it so much
E ven the ghost in Year 4
N ever have I had such a fright or fun.

Rebecca Blair (7)
Eton Wick CE First School, Eton Wick

Romans

R omans tried to invade Britain
O n their chariots
M any of the Celts died
A nd many didn't
'N othing scares us,' said the Romans, 'Boudicca doesn't!'
S ome forts are near Hadrian's Wall!

Humair Munawer (7)
Eton Wick CE First School, Eton Wick

The Lion

A lion is big
A lion is bold
He sits in his cage
Even when it is cold
He roars when he's angry
He stands when he's proud
And he prowls up and down
In front of a crowd.

Jack Steptoe (7)
Eton Wick CE First School, Eton Wick

Teachers

T houghful
E ducational
A rtistic
C reative and clever
H onest
E ver so happy
R eally smart
S miling.

Roopinder Virdee (7)
Eton Wick CE First School, Eton Wick

Babies Crying

Babies crying
Little toddlers screaming
Girls having ice creams
Boys putting on the washing machines
A woman in a wheelchair
Oh, a baby in the air!

Gaganpreet Chana (8)
Eton Wick CE First School, Eton Wick

Autumn

Shiny conkers falling down
Cheeky squirrels burrowing quietly
Brown nuts hidden carefully
Orange pumpkins lit early
Spiky hedgehogs hibernating slowly
Sparkly fireworks zooming rapidly
Crunching leaves floating gently
Golden corn harvested now
Cold wind whistling loudly.

Gaganpreet Chana & Alice Fletcher (8)
Eton Wick CE First School, Eton Wick

The Five Senses Of Autumn

See
Brightly coloured leaves, russet, yellow, orange and green
Tumble to the ground
Red berries on bushes and on the ground.

Touch
Green, rough leaves on all the trees and bushes
Soft, soggy mud as we step on it.

Hear
Crispy, crunchy leaves blow all around us
Hear the leaves rustle across the ground.

Smell
Smell the damp leaves falling off the bushes and trees.

Taste
Taste the food that is cooking in the kitchen.

Remi Georgallis (11)
Fosse Primary School, Leicester

Christmas Is Coming

Here comes Christmas
Buy a cracker and pick a person to pull it
Buy the presents, give them to Santa
Let him deliver them to the houses.

Christmas morning, children wake you up
They want to open their presents and get all excited
They open up their presents
Give you a kiss and hug
How can they ever repay you for giving them so much?

They play with all their presents
Eat all their chocolates
Don't stop playing till the day is done.

Time for Christmas dinner
Eat chicken and veg
Cranberry or apple sauce, finish all your dinner
Get some dessert now, Christmas pudding
If you have a tin of chocolates, give one each
Let them have a great Christmas.

Take your children out somewhere nice
Take them to see their families
If you're alone, don't worry
I'm sure you will still have fun.

Lucy Louise Crisp (10)
Fosse Primary School, Leicester

Tiger Haiku

In the green jungle
I am looking for my prey
It is in the night.

Liam Smith (9)
Fosse Primary School, Leicester

Autumn

Leaves rustling on the trees.
Crunching underneath your feet.
The sound of the wind whistling past your face,
Calling out the name autumn.

The smell of the soggy, damp leaves,
On the trees and on the bushes.

The feel of the cold air against your skin.
The rough, the crunchy and the soggy leaves on the floor.

The red, brown, green, yellow and russet leaves.
The bare branches, the leaves all over the ground,
The berries on the trees.

The taste of all the hot food,
To warm you up.
The berries for the birds to eat.

Charlotte Louise Gallagher (10)
Fosse Primary School, Leicester

Leaves

All the leaves fall off the trees
They blow on the ground wherever they please
When I stand on the leaves they *crunch, crunch, crunch!*
It sounds like when you're in the dinner hall
When you're having your lunch
The leaves are red, yellow and green
They are the crunchiest leaves I've ever seen.

As the leaves rustle around
The crunchy leaves crunch on the ground
Now it is nearly time for winter to come
Then I can play with the snow
And that will be fun!

Cherish Dean (10)
Fosse Primary School, Leicester

Space

When I look up from Earth
I see stars shining
And the moon with its silver lining
Next to Mercury, Venus and Mars.

I peer at the Milky Way up high
And look at Jupiter in the sky
I wish that I could fly
And see right through the halfway moon.

Looking through the window
I see a shooting star
Then I go to bed
And dream of going far.

Still in my dream
In my big spaceship
I see glowing planets
With aliens that live
Then I go home and write a story
Of my whole dream
That's best of them all.

Jorden Deannan Fox (11)
Fosse Primary School, Leicester

Roses Are Red

Roses are red
Violets are blue
I have never seen
Someone as sweet as you
When I am awake
I look for you
When I am asleep
I dream of you
What can I do
When I am missing you?

Catherine Peach (10)
Fosse Primary School, Leicester

Autumn

The leaves are turning from green to red
Now we know Earth is going to bed.

Crunch, rustle, crunch, rustle
All the squirrels are in a bustle.

In my hand the leaves go *crunch!*
I sweep them all up in a bunch.

I can smell all the fresh air
Whip! Whip! Whip! goes my hair.

Crunch! Crunch! Crunch!
Sweet apples I munch.

Rhian Ward (10)
Fosse Primary School, Leicester

Autumn Morning

Leaves crunch, squirrels munch,
Bare trees, cold breeze.

Fresh air on my tongue,
Whistling that autumn song.

You see red, yellow, russet and brown,
You hear that autumn sound.

Camo-green, it makes a scene,
Damp leaves make you sneeze.

Thomas Simpson (10)
Fosse Primary School, Leicester

Snow Tiger - Haiku

A cold snow mountain
A snow tiger searches for
Food for his dinner.

Muhammad Bhawoodin (9)
Fosse Primary School, Leicester

Autumn Days

I can see the cranberry-red
berries on the tree.
I can hear the swaying
leaves as they pass.
I can smell the damp
leaves while walking through the playground.
As I walk, I can hear different sounds.
When I stamp my feet, I can feel
the soggy leaves.

I can smell rotten leaves
while the wind is whistling
through the trees.
I can taste the fresh air
in my mouth.
And I can *shout, shout* and *shout!*
I can see the bare trees and the bark
on the ground.
I can taste the berries.

Leaves on the trees are
turning yellow, brown and red.
I can see the damp
leaves on the ground.
I can smell the harvest
from the bread.
Adding winter is coming from ahead.

Sarata Seisay (10)
Fosse Primary School, Leicester

Spiders - Haiku

In the dark jungle
Spiders scurry in their lairs
On a windy night.

Thomas Arrowsmith (9)
Fosse Primary School, Leicester

A Sad Story

I live in New York
Do you?
There are big buildings
And small ones too.
But to you, they're brand new.

It's horrible when people are beat upon
And people spit on the street
People in bare feet,
Hobos in the street,
Who people don't meet.

Berwick Dawson (9)
Fosse Primary School, Leicester

On Christmas Day

On Christmas Day, snow
Falls on my head.

I hear the Christmas bells,
Ringing in the church.

The fire is lit,
To keep you warm.

The children sing,
The Christmas song at your doors.

Tapiwa Savanhu (10)
Fosse Primary School, Leicester

Dolphin - Haiku

Swims in the ocean
Dolphins glide in the blue sea
In the midday sun.

Katie Allen (9)
Fosse Primary School, Leicester

School Rules

School is cool,
Whatever I say,
If they take the Mick,
They will pay.

At school the food is good,
But really it does *not* taste like mud,
My school is the best,
It is better than the rest.

They take us on trips
And are very kind,
When we can take water or juice, well I take little sips,
If we might spill some and so they say, 'Never mind.'

Sometimes we have a show and tell,
Then we see if we can spell,
When dinner rings we might say, 'Dinner rings to our ears,'
Or, 'Dinner appears.'

When we go home,
I could say, 'Oh wait, but what happened to Rome?'
When I reach home in Mum's car,
I go to bed and then see the same star.

Tyler West (10)
Fosse Primary School, Leicester

Robin In December

When the leaves have fallen
And the days begin to shorten,
When the summer flowers have gone
And we put our warm coats on,
The robin comes back again,
With his red coat on.

Katie Louise Walton Barnes (9)
Fosse Primary School, Leicester

Dreaming

When I close my eyes to sleep,
Into a fantasy I slowly creep,
A world full of fairies and fun,
Close your eyes,
You too can come
And when Mum comes to wake me up,
I hide under the quilt and say, 'Shut up!'

Roísìn Murphy (9)
Fosse Primary School, Leicester

Yellow Belly Custard

Yellow belly custard,
Green snot pie.
Mix them both together,
With a dead dog's eye.
Spread it on a sandwich, nice and thick,
Swallow it down with a cold cup of sick.

Paris Parra-Watson (10)
Fosse Primary School, Leicester

Remember, Remember

Remember, remember the 11th of November,
The soldiers who died in the war.
They were buried in a field where poppies grew,
They ended up dying trying to save you.
Some still live today,
We should never forget the people who died that day.

Ashleigh Giles (10)
Fosse Primary School, Leicester

Fear

Fear is like blood dripping down the stairs
Fear sounds like creaking doors opening and shutting
Fear looks like a black sky at night-time,
Fear feels like someone creeping up at you.
Fear smells like someone lighting a fire.

Liam Murray
Foxes Piece School, Marlow

Hate

It reminds me of a bull charging around a field.
It smells like burning fire
It looks like smelly burning feet.
It feels like a chilli burning in your mouth
It sounds like people screaming when they're right next to me,
Hate is real like a flaming fire in the wood.

Daniel Page (8)
Foxes Piece School, Marlow

Happiness

It reminds me of flowers dropping on the roof.
It smells like rose petals.
It feels like I am flying the sky,
It looks like a white dove in the tree.
Happiness is like a dove flying around.

Victoria Mundy
Foxes Piece School, Marlow

Fear

Fear is red like a burning fire
It reminds me of a rhino getting ready to charge.
It looks like a ghost turning on the tap.
It sounds like a wolf howling at the moonlight
It smells like bacon sizzling in fire
It feels like my head is steaming like a kettle.

Kirsty Walsh (8)
Foxes Piece School, Marlow

Happiness

It falls like fresh air
It looks like braces
It's blue, the colour I like
It sounds like the breeze,
It reminds me of Bratz dolls I like to play with
It smells like my mum's cooking my favourite dinner.

Rosie Edmonds
Foxes Piece School, Marlow

Hate

It feels like a flaming hot body that burns when you touch it
It sounds like ten people shouting and stamping
Hate is black like a burnt tree
It reminds me of a volcano ready to erupt
It smells like a dead body moving in my house
It looks like a little devil that has a tantrum.

Caroline Hester (9)
Foxes Piece School, Marlow

Happiness

It sounds like roses dropping from a rose bush
It looks lie a new surf board on the sea
It reminds me of a lovely, new, shiny bike
It smells like a lovely flower
It feels like a lovely bird flying in the sky,
Happiness is pink like a rose.

Tamara Comley (8)
Foxes Piece School, Marlow

Hate

It sounds like ten people shouting in your head.
It feels like bats flapping their wings.
Hate is black like thunder and lightning
It reminds me of bats and ghosts making funning noises.
It smells like burning fire
It looks like an evil animal.

Kiri Hall
Foxes Piece School, Marlow

Fear

It looks like a creepy crawly tarantula
It feels like a bully fighting me
Fear is blue like a baby crying
It sounds like someone switching your brain off
It reminds me of a headbutting racing rhino.

Michael Sproate (8)
Foxes Piece School, Marlow

Fear

It feels like you're scared and something is going to go wrong
It reminds me of someone or something going to charge
Fear is blue like a cold ice cube
It smells like danger
It looks like a spider climbing up the wall
It sounds like the footsteps of a bully.

Lauren Taylor (8)
Foxes Piece School, Marlow

Fear

It smells like wood on a boiling hot fire,
It sounds like a spooky rhino about to charge
It looks like a scary shadow with horns
It reminds me of a horror film.
Fear is blue like a bit of sky
It feels like a rhino chasing me.

Amber Moore
Foxes Piece School, Marlow

Fear

It reminds me of a charging buffalo about to knock a cat out
It feels like being in a desert on my own with the sun,
It looks like a red kite fighting with a crow
It sounds like a mouse in the house
Fear is grey like a lynx in the woods.
It smells like a dragon flying near the pond.

Frank Alderman (8)
Foxes Piece School, Marlow

Happiness

It smells like mash potatoes in an oven
It reminds me of playing football as soon as possible
It feels like I am going to score a goal
It looks like I have got the question right
It sounds like I won the football match
Happiness is pink like a pig.

Josh Dean (8)
Foxes Piece School, Marlow

Fear

Fear is the colour of black
Fear smells like blood
Fear feels like people screaming
Fear reminds me of screaming all around
Fear looks like people dying
Fear sounds like shouting.

Billie Burns
Foxes Piece School, Marlow

Happiness

Happiness is yellow like the sun
It feels like being snug in bed
It smells like perfume
It looks like smiles
It sounds like playing
It reminds me of friends.

Annabel Ogden (8)
Foxes Piece School, Marlow

Happiness

Happiness is blue like a summer sky
It feels warm
It smells of pretty roses
It sounds like children playing tennis
It looks like flowers
It reminds me of people playing.

Shane Wyatt (7)
Foxes Piece School, Marlow

Happiness

Happiness reminds me of good times in the past,
It looks like you're in Heaven,
Happiness is light not dark,
It feels like you're being a jolly person.
It smells like a scent of a flower.

Sophie Giles
Foxes Piece School, Marlow

Happiness

It feels like the sun shining on me
It smells like a bunch of roses in a field
It reminds me of a baby as cheerful as a flower
It is yellow like the sun
It looks like a baby bird in a nest
It sounds like the sun singing in the morning.

Emma-Louise Foster (10)
Foxes Piece School, Marlow

Happiness

It sounds like a girl singing beautifully.
It smells like a fragrant rose,
It is the colour of a lovely red love heart.
It feels like a lovely hot day.
It looks like a lovely bar of chocolate
It feels like a good day at school.

Ashley Dean (10)
Foxes Piece School, Marlow

Love

Love reminds me of my first kiss
Love smells like a sweet smelly perfume
Love looks like a sunny beach
Love sounds like the big sunny ocean.
Love feels like warmth around me
Love is the colour of deep red roses.

Kelly Buck (11)
Foxes Piece School, Marlow

Happiness

It looks like a smelly, laughing clown
It is red like rosy cheeks
It feels like you are in a rest area.
It smells like a brilliant perfume
It reminds me of a girl planting flowers.
It sounds like a bird singing in the morning.

Ka-Ho Chan (11)
Foxes Piece School, Marlow

Sadness

It reminds me of being left alone
And abandoned when parents have died.
My gran getting old
It looks like a dying leaf falling in winter.
It sounds like someone crying.
It smells like a fire in a church.

Jamie Jones
Foxes Piece School, Marlow

Sadness

It smells like a bonfire in the middle of the night.
It reminds me of my favourite guinea pig dying.
It feels like a nasty cut that I have just got.
It looks like a horrible castle with cobwebs hanging from it.
It sounds like someone standing on rustling leaves.

Hannah Page (10)
Foxes Piece School, Marlow

Sadness

It feels like a damp dingy day
It looks like a rainy miserable day.
It sounds like wind blowing on the shutters
It smells like a horrible landfill sight with lots of rubbish
It reminds me of when Sukie died, that made me sad.

Adam Newson
Foxes Piece School, Marlow

Sadness

It sounds like crying in my mind.
It smells like petrol that makes me sick.
It reminds me of when I'm all alone,
It feels like being stung by a wasp.
It looks like being at a funeral and crying.

Corrina Bignall
Foxes Piece School, Marlow

Fear!

It sounds like a scream in my mind.
It looks like a devil with glowing red eyes.
It smells like an old musty rubbish bin
It feels like a skeleton with wet slimy bones and cracks in its head.

Harry Elliman
Foxes Piece School, Marlow

Happiness

The colour is red like roses.
It feels like love in a bedroom.
It smells like love between people.
It reminds me of love in a field.
It looks like a big smile.
It sounds like romantic songs.

Ben Newson
Foxes Piece School, Marlow

Love

Love feels like warmth and romance
It sounds like the plucking of harp strings
It smells like fresh flowers
The colour looks like deep red roses
It reminds me of a hot bath and lots of flowers.

Mitzi Settle
Foxes Piece School, Marlow

Love

Love is the colour of deep red roses
It feels of warmth all around me
It sounds like the plucking of harp strings
It smells like a sweet smelling perfume
It looks like doves cooing in the leafy branch of a tree.

Laila Lanigan
Foxes Piece School, Marlow

Happiness

It smells like roses in a beautiful garden.
It reminds me of when I stay at my dad's.
It's a red colour like a heart.
It looks like a bright, colourful bumblebee flying.
It feels like a nice warm bath.
It sounds like a smooth romantic dance.

Chloe Ball (10)
Foxes Piece School, Marlow

Love

It is the colour of gold and red roses
It feels like a deep first kiss.
It sounds like the waves beating against the seashore.
It reminds me of a nice hot bath.

Matthew Tipping
Foxes Piece School, Marlow

Anger

Anger looks like an exploding volcano,
Anger reminds me of a red-hot flush,
Anger feels like a revolting, large spot
Anger sounds like pain and violent screams
Anger smells like red, slushy blood
Anger is the colour of dangerous black.

Jasmine Power (10)
Foxes Piece School, Marlow

Happiness

Happiness is orange like the colour of dawn.
Happiness looks like the hot blazing sun.
Happiness sounds like the blue chirping birds.
Happiness feels like two people jumping on soft, bumpy clouds.
Happiness smells like two pink roses wrapped around each other.
Happiness reminds me of my family.

Daniel Moore (10)
Foxes Piece School, Marlow

Anger

Anger is grey like a grey, rainy cloud.
Anger looks like a violent bomb.
Anger reminds me of a broken heart.
Anger smells like some blood dripping off a small boy's face.
Anger sounds like screams and shouts.
Anger feels like a hard, sharp rock.

Michael Ogden (10)
Foxes Piece School, Marlow

Sadness

Sadness is grey as a broken heart
Sadness looks like the tears of the grey, pale clouds
Sadness smells like burning photos
Sadness sounds like children crying
Sadness reminds me of people tearing apart
Sadness feels like devils taking your soul out.

Harry Norton (10)
Foxes Piece School, Marlow

Hate

Hate looks like vicious fighting
Hate sounds like loud screams and shouts
Hate smells like a flaming hot fire
Hate feels like blood dripping on the floor
Hate reminds me of falling out with your best friend
Hate is deep, dark and black, like a thundering sky.

Aislinn Darvell (9)
Foxes Piece School, Marlow

Happiness

Happiness is orange like the burning fire we put on, on cold nights.
Happiness looks like all the colourful fish at the bottom of the sea.
Happiness sounds like dolphins squealing joyfully in cold, salty water.
Happiness feels like hot, melting chocolate round your mouth.
Happiness reminds me of my family.

Georgina Harper (9)
Foxes Piece School, Marlow

Sadness

Sadness is black like a shredded heart
Sadness sounds like one million babies crying and screaming
Sadness looks like the greyest sky
Sadness smells like the biggest, blazing hot fire in Hell
Sadness reminds me of terrible pain and ghostly screams
Sadness feels like walking on a mile of burning hot ashes.

Patrick Castle (9)
Foxes Piece School, Marlow

Anger

Anger is red like thick, runny blood
Anger looks like an erupting volcano
Anger reminds me of a disastrous tantrum
Anger sounds like a thunderous roar
Anger smells like a blazing inferno
Anger feels like the world turning upside down.

Sayma Rob (10)
Foxes Piece School, Marlow

Sadness

Sadness is grey like a rainy day
Sadness looks like people crying when they are hurt.
Sadness smells like dog food
Sadness sounds like thunder and lightning
Sadness feels like breaking hearts
Sadness reminds me of a baby hamster that is lost.

Esther Williams (10)
Foxes Piece School, Marlow

Hate

Hate looks like the big dark clouds
Hate smells of hot burning coals
Hate feels like hard kicks
Hate reminds me of going to school
Hate is grey like grey miserable mornings.

Jack Smith
Foxes Piece School, Marlow

Hate

Hate smells like burning wood
Hate looks like dark black smoke
Hate is grey like a thundery sky
Hate sounds like people screaming for help
Hate feels like a punch
Hate reminds me of dripping blood.

Harry Scrace
Foxes Piece School, Marlow

Hate

Hate looks like a bad storm
Hate smells like smoke
Hate sounds like a wolf growling in the dark forest.
Hate feels like people hitting you.
Hate reminds me of shopping
Hate is black like a dark cloud.

Dominic Lai
Foxes Piece School, Marlow

Anger

It sounds like me arguing with my friends.
It remind me of wrestling.
It looks like fighting.
It smells like blood.
It feels nasty and horrible.
Anger is grey like clouds.

Ashley Lanigan
Foxes Piece School, Marlow

Happiness

Happiness is yellow like the sun
It sounds like a child playing happily
It smells like cut grass
It looks like the sun
It reminds me of a sunny day
It feels like the warm sunshine

Georgina Giles
Foxes Piece School, Marlow

Anger

Anger is red like fire
It feels horrible
It reminds me of blood
It looks like lightning and rain in the darkness
It smells like hot flames
It sounds cross.

Ryan Haas (8)
Foxes Piece School, Marlow

Sadness

Sadness is blue like a stormy sky
It looks like tears.
It reminds me of bullies
It sounds like babies crying
It feels like hailstones
It smells like old dogs.

Rebecca Jones
Foxes Piece School, Marlow

Sadness

Sadness is blue like the sky
It looks like tears
It reminds me of bullies
It sounds like people crying
It feels like rain
It smells like the trees.

Summayyah Shah (7)
Foxes Piece School, Marlow

Fear

Fear reminds me of blood dripping down the doors
Fear smells like vinegar
Fear feels like my mum's hand touching me to wake up
Fear looks like the black sky at night-time.

Chantelle Bennett (8)
Foxes Piece School, Marlow

Hate

The colour of hate is black
It sounds like crying
It feels sad
It looks like angry people.
It smells like my brother.
It reminds me of sharks.

Leanne Dix
Foxes Piece School, Marlow

Hate

Hate is black like a storm
It sounds like a big bang
It smells like dead flowers
It feels like there is a big, bad storm coming
It looks like black clouds
It reminds me of people shouting at each other.

Danielle Lovett (7)
Foxes Piece School, Marlow

Sadness

Sadness is blue like the sky
It smells like tears
It feels like being lonely
It sounds like sad music
It looks like people crying
It reminds me, I want my mum and dad.

Perri Miller
Foxes Piece School, Marlow

Fear

Fear is black like the dark
It smells like the blood of a vampire
It feels very scary
It reminds me of skeleton bones
It looks like blood
It sounds like screaming.

Connor Bignall
Foxes Piece School, Marlow

Hate

Hate is black like a night sky
It feels like thunder
It makes me angry
It smells like cold air
It sounds like breaking glass.

Jessica Hunter (8)
Foxes Piece School, Marlow

My Wonderful World

The Earth is so big
The Earth is so large
No one can lift it but my auntie Marge.
It is so big, it is so beefy
Looking at it makes me sleepy.
This is a puzzle I ponder about . . .
If it's moving so fast why doesn't it knock us out?
I can't always see it, I can't always feel it,
Still I keep on trying.
The wonders of the Earth prevent me from crying.
I wish I knew more mysteries of our beautiful planet
Living, dying, loving, trying.

Roisin Flannery (10)
Gig Mill Primary School, Stourbridge

Miss Collis

M iss Collis is lovely like a beautiful bird
'I s she?' - 'Yes, well that's what I heard'
S he loves everyone and says
'S tart to dance, the fun's begun.' Miss . . .

C ollis is cool and she's the best
O ne of the things I love is how she's dressed
L ove is her big thing, she knows a lot,
L ove of life and fun she's got
I f she's the one for you put your name in her . . .
S lot!

Mairead Flannery (8)
Gig Mill Primary School, Stourbridge

Autumn

Conkers fall off the trees,
They shine and look the same.
Look at them lying there.
Berries for birds,
Blue and red,
I like autumn.

Tonicha Massam (6)
Gilberdyke Primary School, Gilberdyke

Not Now Nigel

Not now Nigel,
You're putting on your vest,
We don't have time to discuss your spelling test.
Not now Nigel,
I thought the staffroom door was locked,
Who knows what you're doing here,
Besides you should have knocked.
Not now Nigel,
Your tea is almost done,
Your hands are still dirty and what's happened to your thumb.
Not now Nigel,
I can hear your sister crying,
Does your thumb still hurt,
No, I don't think you're dying.
Not now Nigel,
I'm putting you to bed,
Please stop wriggling,
Of course that's your real head
Not now Nigel,
It's the middle of the night,
Everyone's still sleeping,
No don't turn on the light!

Abigail Jackson (9)
Grayshott CE Primary School, Hindhead

River

River, river flowing far,
Left and right the way I turn,
Walk, trot, canter,
As fast as I can go,
A man diving
A bird gliding,
Fierce lions playing,
The engine of a car

The scent of blooming flowers,
Fish like darting arrows,
Hitting the board,
A rocket launching,
A stone falling into the water,
Like a plane landing

The river is like a patterned blanket,
Weed growing,
A crab peeping

The river will never die,
Like you and me,
Its memories will never go,
Like mine and yours,
The river will always be there,
Not like you and me.

Shona Morrison (10)
Grayshott CE Primary School, Hindhead

The River

Like a slithering snake
Leaping lions.
As if it were a fighting fox,
Dancing deer.
A flickering candle in the moonshine
The fish are a sparkling hailstorm
But then comes the crash of waves and we know we must die.

Chris Jacobs (9)
Grayshott CE Primary School, Hindhead

Christmas

It's Christmas time,
There's frost on the ground,
Love and joy are to be found.
Children with carols are singing,
With the Christmas bells ringing.

Mary and Joseph are walking afar,
They're looking for a place to stay,
The journey leads to a stable that has lots of hay,
Mary had a baby called Jesus, who in the hay he did lay.

Up in the sky was a very bright star,
That could be seen from afar
The three wise men travelled several nights,
With gifts for baby Jesus, who was a lovely sight.

Christmas time is a time for giving and sharing,
Allowing people to show they are caring,
It is a time that we all love,
And share with God above.

Emily Rabstein (7)
Grayshott CE Primary School, Hindhead

When The Wind Blows

When the wind blows,
Outside is a battle,
Inside is a rattle,
The wind blows to the north,
South, east and west in the silent sun.

So the north wind blows
Like a feather in the wind it runs
Around the cities or towns
Like a traveller running a world.

Benjamin Johnston (9)
Grayshott CE Primary School, Hindhead

The Scents And Pongs

Dog food, what a whiff when you sniff
Cabbage cooking in the pot - really smelly, really hot,
Gone off cheese makes you sneeze,
Public toilets what a reek, not been cleaned for a week,
Egg sandwiches what a pong, think I'm eating them,
You're wrong!
Bonfire's horrid, smelly smoke, in a minute I will choke
Yuck . . . smells bad!

Melted chocolate in a cake, a taste so yummy, smells so great,
Fresh baked bread in the shop smells so good I'll take the lot,
Most people think petrol does pong,
But me, I think that they are wrong,
Perfume sprayed just once or twice, makes my neck smell very nice,
Rose petals smell so sweet, makes your garden so complete,
Breathe in the fresh sea air, feel the breeze as it blows your hair.
Mmm . . . smells good!

Nicky Houghton (10)
Grayshott CE Primary School, Hindhead

Silver Moon

The silver moon walks round the world
As bright as a light,
She is shining brightly as she walks in fright,
She swerves her silver dress as she dances like a kite,
As she dances she lifts off in flight,
When she flies she sees the city with lights so bright,
She goes down to Earth and walks round all night,
When the sun comes up she runs away
Because it's too bright and she flies far, far *away!*

Rachel Phillips (9)
Grayshott CE Primary School, Hindhead

Moonlight Garden

In the dark and gloomy garden,
With dustbin bags rattling in the wind.
A rare ghost following behind you,
Tapping on the shoulder.
Litter lapping round you, lamp post sparkling
On the old, dusty, gloomy garden.
The way the moon shines through the window
Reflecting onto the pool.
Owls hooting, echoing through the midnight sky.
White and dusty wings flapping in the
Glittering but gloomy sky.
The way the stars sparkle in time
With the shooting stars.
Moonlight garden.

Abby Hutchins (9)
Grayshott CE Primary School, Hindhead

River

The river rushes ruffle,
The water whispers wisely,
And the colours shimmer slowly.

But down below are flickering fish flapping,
And silver sawing sand,
And slimy stones rolling with the flow.

But up on the wall of the river,
A mouldy pipe sticks his green head out,
And spits thick brown water out of his circular mouth.

A beaming blue dragonfly,
Landing on his mouth,
Her wings were like rainbows, flapping in the wind.

Frankie Spice (9)
Grayshott CE Primary School, Hindhead

Uncle Rob

We want to remember our uncle Rob
To some he was known as a good mate Bob,
Always having fun,
Ready for a laugh,
Water splashing everywhere when he had a bath.

He's always in our thoughts and never far away,
He's always watching over us all throughout the day.

And when we go to sleep at night
We always send a kiss
Just to let him know how much he is missed.

Katie Winstanley (8)
Grayshott CE Primary School, Hindhead

Silver

The silver moon drifts the seas.
The light of her shone glints on the trees.
Her light slowly seeps its way
Through every crevice and all the grey.

The garden scattered with sparkling flints.
The night-time grass but with dew it glints
And there lie silver fish by sparkling reeds.

Alec Cramb (10)
Grayshott CE Primary School, Hindhead

Colours

Red is for a rose which shines in the daylight
Yellow is for the stars what twinkle and glitter in the night.
White is for the sparkling white dove that flutters in the daylight.
Blue is for the sparkling waterfall which is so magical.
Silver is for my shimmering eye what twinkle and sparkle and glitter
Green is for the shaking green grass.

Elisha Palmer (9)
Grayshott CE Primary School, Hindhead

Christmas Child

It's coming round to that time of year
When all the people play and cheer
As it's nearly Christmas time you see
For us it's decorations, presents, lights and a tree.

Do you know a poor girl or boy
That we could bring hope and joy
By sending some gifts in 'Love in a Box'
Maybe inside will be a hat, scarf and some socks.

There are countries still at war
And lots and lots of children very poor
Let's all pray for peace this Christmas Day
And hope we treat one another in a special way.

Luca Whiteway (7)
Grayshott CE Primary School, Hindhead

Christmas Time

Christmas is all about having fun
'Happy Christmas,' people say
Reindeers coming with tinkling bells
I love Christmas, so do you
Santa's coming on his sleigh, waiting for his mince pie
Teachers want presents too
Many of us have Christmas dinner
All of us love Christmas
Santa must be busy, busy.

Twinkling lights on the trees
I enjoy Christmas too much, I can't get it off my mind
Meet Santa Claus at the North Pole
Everyone I'm sure gets lots of presents at Christmas time.

Sophie Gatcum (7)
Grayshott CE Primary School, Hindhead

Battlefield

Soldiers on the battlefield, their lives taken away,
But we must remember them on a special day.
Soldiers on the battlefields,
The poppies grow where they lie,
Marking the spot where they died.

Now a few decades on,
Even though they're long gone,
We wear a poppy to remember those people
On the 11th of November.

Tom Gladman (8)
Grayshott CE Primary School, Hindhead

Love

Love is all about
Caring for each other
People at war in hospitals
And people in Africa as well
Love is about looking after your friends.

Love is all about
Jesus and God
Because Jesus died on a cross
And God is the leader of Heaven.

That's what love is all about.

Zoe Marshall (7)
Grayshott CE Primary School, Hindhead

Peace

Peace is when people don't fight in the world,
Peace is when people are friends,
If we never ever have peace in the world,
Then it's probably when the world's gonna end.

Arlen Millward (7)
Grayshott CE Primary School, Hindhead

River

A glimmering, scaly snake
Riding the lifeless wind
A slinky, wiggly worm
Trying to get out of its skin

A wash of blank darkness
Under the water
The fish are helpless
Shore then slaughter

I should get home
To my warm, cosy bed
You need lots of sleep
To refresh your head

All I need to do
Is fall fast asleep
Until tomorrow
They will wait and weep.

Harry Lovelock (9)
Grayshott CE Primary School, Hindhead

River

River, river flowing fast
Can the running water last
Off it goes from the source
Starting on its windy course.

Meandering in and out
There's a minnow and a trout
Into the sea runs the river
It might not be there forever.

Because on a hot day vapour rises
From rivers all shapes and sizes
Into rain clouds raining long
To withstand it you have to be strong.

Nick Wilson (10)
Grayshott CE Primary School, Hindhead

Good Smells Bad Smells

Flowers in the garden,
Fresh cooked gingerbread,
Something from the bakery,
Like fresh cooked bread,
Even homemade cakes,
Sweets that I like to,
Mmm smells good.

Shoes when you've been walking,
Your armpits when you've been sweating,
Your feet are wearing shoes,
Like loads of poo,
And smelly pans,
A green fish tank,
Yuck smells bad.

Theo Gardener (10)
Grayshott CE Primary School, Hindhead

Silver

The smooth silver moonlight,
Lay upon my garden,
She lies upon the delicate frost.

She sounds like crunching crust,
While she secretly steps walking across the frost,
She shivers and stutters,
While her soft silver moonlight runs across my face.

But then the sun comes out so she gets scared,
And she goes to the other side,
Which is a different, dark place.

Meg Phillips (9)
Grayshott CE Primary School, Hindhead

The Christmas Child

'He's been, he's been,' the children say
When they wake up on Christmas Day.

With lots of toys,
For all girls and boys,
Downstairs they run,
Full of joy and fun.

Jesus looked down from Heaven, and smiled,
The Lord is the happiest Christmas child.

Rachel North (8)
Grayshott CE Primary School, Hindhead

I Am A Shoebox

I am a shoebox and I got wrapped up with paper
I have toys inside me
I am very full
The child who filled me tried very hard
To make sure that everything fitted
At Christmas, a child will be waiting for me,
And they will be surprised by the toys that are in me
And know that I came to bring joy and hope.

Bridget Johnston (8)
Grayshott CE Primary School, Hindhead

My Memories

Up there there's someone special,
Up above the stars,
Where God keeps all his special people,
As our memories.

My cousin called Lachlan is dead now,
He died in a hospital with an illness
But lucky me, I got to see him once.

Millie Whittam (8)
Grayshott CE Primary School, Hindhead

Smells

Foreign food now that's quite nice
But not as nice as a chocolate slice.

A slice of fresh bread with butter
Is great tucker.

A nice big cookie and all things nice
Home-made cakes in the shape of mice.

Mmm . . . smells nice.

Bad eggs on burnt toast
Makes me feel like a ghost.

Pepperoni and macaroni
I would rather be lonely.

Diesel oil and burnt plastic
Neither makes me feel fantastic

Yuck smells bad!

Daniel Manners (10)
Grayshott CE Primary School, Hindhead

Peace Is All We Want

Christmas is all about caring,
But mostly sharing.

To bring love and joy,
To every girl and boy.

To shine a light,
Through their night.

To help them live,
We all must give.

A simple smile,
Could carry them a mile.

To bring peace and hope,
Into their hearts.

Harry New (7)
Grayshott CE Primary School, Hindhead

My Dog Jake

Jake was big, brown and hairy
His bark was loud, clear and scary
Mummy hated these noises
But I loved his voices
Barking when the doorbell pealed
Whining when he wanted a meal
His hair and paw marks got everywhere
On our socks and on his chair
When we took him for walks
He jumped over tree trunks and rocks
He looked like a Rottie
But was really a softy
He was fourteen years old
Still brave and bold
Now he's up in Heaven
Thinking he's only seven!

Josh McIvor (8)
Grayshott CE Primary School, Hindhead

Pudsey

Pudsey is a bear
Who's full of love and care
He's also very rare
With lots of yellow hair.

If you see him on the street
Be sure you go and greet
This bear who's very sweet
And it'll be a treat.

He helps unlucky girls and boys
He provides them with lovely new toys
He's not a bear you have to feed
He's the mascot of 'Children in Need'.

Holly Maynard (8)
Grayshott CE Primary School, Hindhead

My Grandad

I have a grandad
Who is a postman
He rides around in
A big red van.

He has a grey beard
And can sometimes be
A bit weird.

He likes to have
A bit of a laugh
And we like to splash him
When we're in the bath.

He likes a bit of opera
And some pop - hoorah!

Rabbie McGowan (8)
Grayshott CE Primary School, Hindhead

Millie

Can we take Millie to school?
No she's too small
Can we take Millie to Legoland?
No she's too small
Can we take Millie to swimming lessons?
No she's too small
Can we take Millie to the cinema?
No she's too small
Can we take Millie to bed?
No she's a *dog!*

Thomas Edser (7)
Grayshott CE Primary School, Hindhead

The Beach

Big waves smash against the sandy shore
White horses push the surfers along
Bringing cries of joy
'Yeah'

Small castles stand fighting the high tide
Sunbathers feel the sun burning into them
Bounce, bounce from the tennis players
Seagulls swooping overhead

Screams as the feet go into the freezing water
Little ones jumping over the waves
The smell of barbecues floods the beach
As the sun goes down between the trees.

Therese O'Neill (10)
Grayshott CE Primary School, Hindhead

The Moon

Glowing orb,
Mystic ball,
For decades the moon has excited all.

Cold light,
In the night,
But always you are burning bright.

Floating high,
In the sky,
I won't be afraid as darkness draws nigh.

Glowing orb,
Mystic ball,
For decades the moon has excited all.

Matthew Phillips (11)
Grayshott CE Primary School, Hindhead

Good Smells, Bad Smells

Good smells are
Like cooked bread
Bad smells are
Like smelly trainers

Good smells are
Like flowers in a garden
Bad smells are like
Smelly clothes on the floor

Good smells are
Like washed clothes
Bad smells are
Like smelly hair

Good smells are
Like fresh air
Bad smells are
Like a green fish tank

Good smells are
Like home-made cakes
Bad smells are
Like fox pooh.

Good smells are
Like hot chocolate
Bad smells are
Like smelly pans.

Lucy Davis (10)
Grayshott CE Primary School, Hindhead

No Scents

How would I know dinner was cooking?
How would I know the fire was burning?
How would I know the cake was cooking?
How would I know you had brought me flowers?
I'm glad I can smell!

Jessica Topping (10)
Grayshott CE Primary School, Hindhead

Remembrance Poem

My great uncle Harry was a talented man
He played a shiny trumpet
In a big brass band.

He spent his time in the Second World War
Out in the heart of Africa
Entertaining all the troops
And their Commanding Officer
But his job was not fun
As some days were spent in the jungle with his gun
But luckily for us when all the fighting had been done
He returned to his home in London.

My mum has told me this story of Great Uncle Harry
And how he is part of our wonderful family
Great Uncle Harry died before I was born
But his memory and stories will remain for evermore.

Jason Banks (8)
Grayshott CE Primary School, Hindhead

My Brother

My brother was nice, my brother was kind
The best brother you ever could find
He would look out for me; he'd help if I was sore
Until the day he banged my head, on the glass in my front door!

My head went bash
The glass went smash,
Mum and Dad went really mad
And said that Nick was very bad.

It was a blip, but it was bad
He's my big brother and I'm not glad!

Alex Wilson (8)
Grayshott CE Primary School, Hindhead

Pongs

Dog poo, dog poo so squishy and brown
Dog poo, dog poo you make me frown.
Shoes, shoes you smell so bad
Shoes, shoes my nose isn't glad.
Cows, cows you don't smell good
Cows, cows you don't smell as I thought you would.
Pears, pears so sticky and sweet
Pears, pears not so tasty to eat.
Old milk, old milk floating and yellow
Old milk, old milk unfortunately I gave you to my old fellow (oops)
Nappies, nappies you live under the kitchen sink
Nappies, nappies you absolutely stink.

Abbi Fisher (10)
Grayshott CE Primary School, Hindhead

Love In A Box

In other countries there are lots of girls and boys,
Who, at Christmas time, aren't given any toys.
Because we know Christmas is a special time for caring
We fill a box with all the things that we don't mind sharing.
The children don't have any presents and are feeling very sad,
Then, at Christmas time, the boxes come
And it makes them very glad.

Billy Spice (7)
Grayshott CE Primary School, Hindhead

Friendly Freddie

Freddie was a friendly dog always by my side.
When we had a meal you could always feel, Freddie by your side.
Always ready for a walk whatever the weather,
Through many puddles and the mud Freddie was a friendly dog.

Christian Manners (8)
Grayshott CE Primary School, Hindhead

Christmas Time

What do I think of at Christmas time?
Spending time with my family and feeling fine.

Lots of presents under the tree.
Lots of presents for you and me.

But what about the people who are cold and alone,
Without any presents, family or home.

Spend time at Christmas thinking of others,
Not just your friends, sisters and brothers.

Talia Harrison (7)
Grayshott CE Primary School, Hindhead

Capital Cross Stitch

C hloe starts with a capital
A nd so does Abbi,
P ig does as well,
I ncluding igloo too.
T om, Tim and Therese do,
A nd so does
L ucy too.

Chloe Gatcum (10)
Grayshott CE Primary School, Hindhead

Lyme Regis

Soft smooth sand,
Loud brass bands.

Bumpy waves,
Sheep that graze.

Fish and chip shop,
Crowded dock.

Lyme Regis!

Lucianna Cole (10)
Grayshott CE Primary School, Hindhead

The Sun

The sun is a
Blazing ball,
A shining light,
And hides every night.

The sun is a
Giant light,
In the shimmering light,
And is beyond my sight.

The sun is a
Flaring ball,
A glimmering sight,
And is my favourite sight,
That gives me might.

Sam Tanswell (10)
Grayshott CE Primary School, Hindhead

Our Fish Fred

Our fish Fred is dead
We put him under the soil for his bed
He lived up to nine years and our eyes were full of tears.
And we miss him very much
But he's gone now so we can't bring him back
But we are very sad.

Claire Delaney (9)
Grayshott CE Primary School, Hindhead

My Grandad

My grandad used to fly up, up in the sky
He liked to dig the garden but mainly when it was dry,
Birdwatching he liked and might sketch a flight
He went fishing now and again but never got a bite.
I'll remember him forever every day and every night.

Rebecca White (8)
Grayshott CE Primary School, Hindhead

Josh

Sometimes granny has Josh to stay
He's a dog who loves to romp and play
We get in the car ready for a walk
Josh whines so loud we can hardly talk
He loses his sticks from time to time
Some up in trees, which we cannot climb
He loves it when we throw the stick into Waggoners Wells
But when he comes out phew! he really does smell
He has to be washed down with the garden hose
But he really hates it when it touches his nose
When he goes home we are very upset
We love him so much he's like our very own pet.

Jo Marshall (9)
Grayshott CE Primary School, Hindhead

Grandad

My grandad sat in his corner chair
And I would hold his hand
He was always there to cheer me up
And made me feel quite grand
I never wanted him to go
It's sad we had to part
I remember him with lots of love
He's always in my heart.

Alexandra Dixon (8)
Grayshott CE Primary School, Hindhead

My Uncle Arthur

My uncle Arthur, who lived in Switzerland
My uncle Arthur, who sadly died long ago.
My uncle Arthur that I can still remember
My uncle Arthur, who I wished was still alive.

Alice Cundy (9)
Grayshott CE Primary School, Hindhead

Hunger

Hunger is brown like bowls with no food,
Hunger smells like air without the scent of food,
Hunger sounds like a rumbling tummy,
Hunger looks like a plate without any food,
Hunger feels like pain,
Hunger tastes like a dry mouth.

Thomas Fox (9)
Longroyde Junior School, Rastrick

What Am I?

I can be blue
I can be white,
And I come out at night
You won't find me in a farm,
Some types of me can do you harm
What am I?

(Answer: Chameleon)

Joe Hollingworth (8)
Mangotsfield CE Primary School, Emersons Green

Football

I like football
I whacked my head on the wall
I kicked the ball
I walked home from school
I dribbled the ball to football and back
I kicked the ball at home
And rang my friend on the phone
And went home.

Amy Willcox (8)
Mangotsfield CE Primary School, Emersons Green

The Animal Party

There was a young dog,
That was sat on a log,
Eating some cake,
By the lake, on a blue plate,
Another 15 mins late,
Came along to the party,
He had a tie, his name Marty,
A puppy, a kitten,
And a mouse,
A snail brought its house,
A dog with a cape
Another weird looking shape,
One was scary,
Another hairy,
And the last, with a flask!

Maria Matias-Lopes (8)
Mangotsfield CE Primary School, Emersons Green

The Mouse And The Boy

I saw a little boy
That was full of joy
He saw a little mouse
In his house
Who said, 'What a lovely toy'
The mouse had louse
In his cat house
Then the boy had a madhouse
In his doghouse
So that's the end of the mouse and the boy.

Ellesse Pearce (8)
Mangotsfield CE Primary School, Emersons Green

God's Creatures

In my ear I hear
The crickets churp
In happy pairs
The butterflies fly
I find the spiders
Hiding in the web
In the air
I find the fly flying
The best thing of all creatures
They've all amazing features.

Hannah Sands (8)
Mangotsfield CE Primary School, Emersons Green

Animals

A greedy hamster ate cake
The zebra drank from a lake
The mouse gathered cheese
A cat caught some peas
The caterpillars were crunching crunchy leaves
They haven't got sleeves.
None of them drink from jugs
Baby lions are called cubs.
Reindeers prance
None of them have pants.

Abbi Wheeler (8)
Mangotsfield CE Primary School, Emersons Green

A Poem About The Sea

Sailing, swinging, wonderful sea,
Shining, silky, blue sea
Rough, wary, calm sea,
Shining, beautiful silver sea,
Golden seaweedy, green sea,

Fishy, sharky, heavy sea
Shingley, pebbly, rocky sea,
Shelly, weedy, dolphiny sea
Sandy, stony, glittering sea,
Multicoloured fishy sea,

Salty, dark, bluey sea
Roaring, rolling, sparkling sea
Grey, scary, dark sea,
Mysterious, islandy, shadowy sea
Rising in a high tide sea
Lowering at a low tide sea.

I just love the sea!

Megan Jones (7)
Portishead Primary School, Portishead

My Friend's Crab

We are two friendly crabs
We don't do a lot
Our best game is nip fight
Our names are Eric and Fred
Sometimes Fred wins but Eric wins the most
We are two friends we don't do a lot.

Ryan Kensit (8)
Riddings Junior School, Riddings

Rabbit

Rabbit, rabbit, rabbit
Funny, fast, furry rabbit
Small, silly, smart rabbit
Rabbit, rabbit, rabbit.

Reagan Withers (7)
St Gregory's Primary School, Longton

Victorian Times

Victorian times are hard, always getting up early,
I think I will get paid today
Cakes and cups I'm selling today
Ten pence I got yesterday
'Oh, here is a customer,' I say to myself
Run over please and buy something from me
I got some money, he bought a cake
And got a cup then ran off like a rake
Now I can go home and start all over again.

The sweeping is sore on the back
I work all day until the woollier stops
My brother is on the mops
End of the day, shillings for pay, go to bed and
Sleep to the next day.

Laurence Killen (10)
St Joseph's Primary School, Crossgar

Panther

Panther, panther - it's jet-black
It speeds past a car
Growls as loud as a trumpet
And it's as black as the night sky.

Marlon Pavanello (9)
St Joseph's Primary School, London

Playtime

Walking in the playground
I can hear children screaming,
Like a mouse about to be hit with a mop.

Walking in the playground
I can see children running
Like dogs chasing a terrified cat.

Walking in the playground
I can feel teachers' hands,
As cold as shivering ice in the North Pole.

Walking in the playground
I can smell the fresh air,
As clean as the whitest snow on top of the French Alps.

Walking in the playground
I can taste the air
As fresh as cool water from a mountain spring.

Walking in the playground
I can hear children crying
Like people sobbing at a funeral

Walking in the playground
I can see boys shooting balls into the goal,
Like birds zooming through the air,
Trying to catch their prey.

Walking in the playground
I can feel the warmness of my jumper
Comforting like the hug from my mother.

Ashleigh Joyce (9)
St Joseph's Primary School, London

The Monkey - Haiku

Monkeys like to climb
Also have feet like their hands
Also like to eat.

Reggie Tomlin (9)
St Joseph's Primary School, London

Feeling Lonely

In the playground,
I stand alone,
Looking at children playing together.
But me
I'm new,
I don't have any friends here.
I stand cold in the corner,
Like an ice block
I see the teacher walking to the line,
Like a bear rushing to get honey.
Now I wait until home time.

Skye Jones (8)
St Joseph's Primary School, London

The Ghost Teacher

Once there was a ghost teacher
She was very, very scary indeed
She used to slither around the school
As if a cheetah was chasing her.
The children at the end of the day
Would run out as fast as they could!
The caretaker was really frightened by the ghost,
Just like everyone else!
Every night she was as cold as ice,
Like a frozen ice cube.

Gayle Tobin (8)
St Joseph's Primary School, London

Help Me!

Squashed in a corner
Big rough boys coming over
Someone please help me!

Ellis Neagle (9)
St Joseph's Primary School, London

I Love To Read

I love to read books
It is so much fun
When I go to my local library
I take every single one.

My favourite author's Jacqueline Wilson
She writes a lot of books
So when I step in my library
I'm so tempted to look.

For example

Ellie from Girls In Love
She's fat, she's plump, quite quiet
She has two best friends
I'm surprised she doesn't go on a diet.

Ayodunni Nuga (9)
St Joseph's Primary School, London

Friends

Friends are helpful
Friends tell secrets
Friends are the best.

Friends all around me
Friends are forever
Friends are joyful
Friends are peaceful.

Genet Gezhay (9)
St Joseph's Primary School, London

Monday Soccer Blues - Haiku

Fouling growling shot
Red card, take a penalty
Chrome boots hit the ball.

Kevin Badejo (9)
St Joseph's Primary School, London

Tiger, Tiger

Tiger, tiger burning bright
As glib as a cat
Amber as the sun
Flickering raven dark stripes.

Tiger, tiger burning bright
Eyes as red as gore
Rapid as a car
What hand dare the sieve of fire.

Raphael Afeniford (9)
St Joseph's Primary School, London

Love

Love is so magical, your eyes twinkle like stars
Love is so romantic full of lots of bliss
Love is to worship and cherish and for honesty
Love is real happiness also joy
Love is for people to treasure
Love is all about truth also have faith
Love is about sharing and caring
Love is a gift from God.

Kevin Badejo (8) & Diana Adelaja (9)
St Joseph's Primary School, London

Secret Of Love And Friendship

Soft sweetness they can never break us up
From baby to child to adult
Oh the joy that is between us
From the summer morn when we were born
Through the mellowing years as we grew up.

But now we are older our friendship has gone
She found a new friend called Sidney
And I'm abandoned alone.

Uyi Ilenbs (9)
St Joseph's Primary School, London

Sports Day

Sports day, sports day, it is such fun,
I never want to end all the runs.
I never like to lose a match,
In the javelin I won't lose a catch.

My friends are filled with delight,
When I won the matches,
I was filled with gold bright
And I got all my catches.

All my enemies, very angry at me,
They never knew they were going to be,
They always wanted to win sports day,
They thought they were going to win today.

My friends nearly won their matches,
It's because they lost one of their catches.
They only won sports day once,
They won by only ten runs.

Ejikeme Iroegbu (7)
St Joseph's Primary School, London

Sabre Teeth - Haikus

Roars in bravery
Smells refreshing scent of prey
With its clashing claws.

The goldish tiger
Roars hungrily, scent, rumour
Wilderness hider.

Gruesome Wrestly
Bristly fur, cave seeker,
No prey, wait next day.

Emmanuel Blango (9)
St Joseph's Primary School, London

My Football Team

When I'm on the football pitch
I kick the ball and it blazes in like a trail of fire.
When I'm on the football pitch
I feel the blood dripping down my face,
Like a waterfall.
When I'm on the football pitch
The spit shoots out of my mouth
Like a cannonball.
When I take a free kick
It is as fast as a shotgun bullet.
When I touch the grass it is wet,
And feels like it has just been watered.
The fans watch me, going wild
Like crazy monkeys swinging in the trees.
I can hear big muddy boots
Smashing on the ground
Like stampeding elephants.

Luke Penn (8)
St Joseph's Primary School, London

My Teacher

Here I am in my classroom
Listening to my teacher teaching.
I can hear my teacher's pen.
Scribbling like the sound of a dog burying a bone.
In the morning I always see my teacher,
Drinking out of her cup,
Like a cat gulping its milk.
My teacher always puts on perfume,
It smells as delicious as flowers,
Spreading their scent in spring.
My teacher reads like a scientist making her notes.
I like my teacher!

Catherine Urbano (8)
St Joseph's Primary School, London

My Best Friend Natasha

I am playing in the playground
Playing a game of 'It' with my best friend
I can hear people running and running
We are as fast as cheetahs chasing their prey.

My best friend Natasha is caring and sweet.
She is as lovely as a deer
Sweet like the smell of dandelions
She smells like strawberry cream.

Natasha's cheeks are as soft as chocolate
Melting in the oven
When I touch Natasha's skin it feels
As smooth as clear water
Her hair is silky like satin.

We like playing in the playground Natasha and me!

K'Shayne Best (8)
St Joseph's Primary School, London

Teachers

While I sit in the classroom
I can hear teachers shouting at children
Loudly like dogs barking.

While I sit in the classroom,
I can hear teachers fighting wildly.
Like two hyenas fighting over a bone

While I sit in the classroom,
I can see my teacher smiling,
Like a clown making jokes.

While I sit in the classroom
I can smell my teacher's perfume
Ripe like a strawberry.

Shannon Tolster (9)
St Joseph's Primary School, London

Wayne Rooney

He is great at football playing with the best teams
He scores loads of goals sometimes he can be very mean
He's so great I wish I could be like him.

His shots are so hard like a cannonball
Destroying everything in front of him
He is really young, only eighteen very small and quite thin
He is such a fierce footballer I'd like to be like him.

Thomas Beaumont (9)
St Joseph's Primary School, London

Wayne Rooney

Dream player
Hat-trick hero
World Cup dreamer
World class striker
Greedy player
Free kick taker.

Young player
Champions League dreamer
Great at long shots.

Siem Efrem (9)
St Joseph's Primary School, London

Christmas Eve

There once was a boy called Steve
Who lived with his mother Neve
One night he said,
'I'm going to bed.'
'But you can't go to bed'
His mother then said
''Cause darling it's Christmas Eve.'

Kerrie Child (9)
St Joseph's Primary School, London

Football

Sometimes is glorious
Sometimes is sad
One team's victorious
One team's unglad.

Sometimes it gets racist
When one team starts to lose
On fighting they might insist
If the supporters stay off the booze.

The players come off the pitch
The supporters still chanting
They turn it into a ditch
The supporters are not inviting.

At full time the winners say 'yeah!'
The losers say 'boo!'
Arsenal and they tear
Millwall get flushed down the loo.

Jonathan Da Costa-Reid (9)
St Joseph's Primary School, London

The Sea

Sea - big, blue, wavy
In the sea comes, it's navy
Sea - big and crashy
The sea fun and splashy.

Sea - fine and sandy
Sea waves as frothy as shandy
On the sea in a boat
In the sea you can float.

In the sea you need to be tough
The sea is kinda rough
The sea's very frothy
The sea's like a cold cup of coffee.

Sam Pascoe (10)
St Joseph's Primary School, London

Football

When I'm kicking the ball it shoots high into the air,
Like a rocket shooting into space.
When I'm wearing my football boots,
I run so fast like Sonic the Hedgehog.
When I'm kicking the ball,
I'm like David Beckham,
Taking a fantastic free kick against France.
When I take my corner it spins in the air,
Like a cartwheel and whips itself in.
If you want to foul me you better be warned
Because my body is as hard as iron.

I am the best footballer in the world.

Benny Uchehara (8)
St Joseph's Primary School, London

Football Pitch

The boy was kicked in the face,
The blood streamed down
Like a river on his frown
The children fell over
Like they had been shot,
They never get hot because
There's always rain,
It's such a pain when we're stuck in the rain.

Daniel Davis (8)
St Joseph's Primary School, London

Cheetah - Haiku

Delightful and fast
Wild, golden cats from Asia
Cat searches its prey.

Henry Frimpong (9)
St Joseph's Primary School, London

School Dinners

I can smell the sweet food
Climbing up the stairs,
Like a rock climber climbing a mountain,
I'm wishing it was twenty-past twelve,
So that it is lunchtime,
I can't wait to eat.
I can taste the bitter vinegar
In my mouth, on my chips,
Like sour boiled sweets.
Fizzing on my tongue.
I love school dinner custard,
It is as beautiful as a butterfly,
Flying in the classroom.

The knife and fork cold on my hand
Like a block of ice,
I can feel the beans
Slipping between my fingers
Like water dripping from a tap.

Billy Day (9)
St Joseph's Primary School, London

Friends

I see children playing happily,
Just like kittens playing with a ball of string.

I hear children playing excitedly
And having fun like children dancing at a party.

I can feel a hand touch me
As soft as rabbit's fur.

I can hear my friends laughing
As loud as a balloon popping.

I can see my friends helping each other
Like a mum caring for her children.

Samantha Obwona (9)
St Joseph's Primary School, London

Running

Running is my best sport,
It makes me fit and healthy.
It makes me want to shout out loud,
That I love running.

When I'm running,
The wind blows through my hair
And the coldness of the weather,
Stings my eyes.

Sometimes I lose,
Sometimes I win,
Either way I'm not in shame,
Because I love running anyway.

Jumoke Akinsola (11)
St Joseph's Primary School, London

The Love That People Give

If someone comes over to you it feels like a dream
But sometimes they just leave you
Like you are trapped in a dark house,
You would feel lonely
But when you go into a snugly, warm house
It's the best dream ever.

Megan Carter (9)
St Joseph's Primary School, London

I Love To Go To School

I love to go to school
On a summer morn
Then go outside with my friends
When the bell rings
It's time to go inside.
And to do some fantastic things.

Gemma Pink (9)
St Joseph's Primary School, London

School Dinner Senses

In school dinners I can hear children whispering to their friends,
Like mice underneath the floorboards.

In school dinners I can taste the food crashing against my teeth,
Like a huge wave crashing onto the shore.

In school dinners I can feel the knife and fork,
Cold metal, I stab the fork into the food and pop it into my mouth.

In school dinners I can see the children crying
because they are in trouble,
Like monkeys all alone who have lost their mother.

In school dinners I can smell the food
whooshing into my nose,
Like a train into a tunnel!

In school dinners I can taste the water in my mouth,
My mouth is a cupboard full of cups and plates.

In school dinners I can hear teachers shouting,
Like a really big alarm clock ringing loudly in my ear.

Jesselle Romero (9)
St Joseph's Primary School, London

A Big Football Pitch

Hearing the fans shouting,
Like 200,000 elephants stampeding on the pitch,
So loud as the teams shout at each other
As loud as they can.

See the ball flying into the goal.
Like the fastest eagle going into the net just so fast.
I cannot believe that it went that fast.

Smelling the burning of the fireworks
Like the smoke from a gun that has just shot a rabbit
Tasting the cold air is like drinking iced water.

Luke Perryman (8)
St Joseph's Primary School, London

My Wonderful Friends

I am in the playground
I can hear my friends laughing
Like witches cackling
At jokes that are not funny.

I am playing with my friend's hair
It is soft and silky
Like a polar bear's fur.
It is long and lovely.

We are all chatting loudly
Like lions roaring in the wild,
We all are chatterboxes.

The playground is cold
And my friends shiver.
Like jelly on a plate.
Their breath is cold and fresh
Like the smell of freshly picked mint.

Hollie Burke (9)
St Joseph's Primary School, London

Childhood Football

I'm on the football pitch
I can hear children shouting
Loudly like a fire bell
Ringing in my ears.

I'm on the football pitch
I can see children playing
Like tigers chasing their prey.

I'm on the football pitch
I see children running
As fast as a racing car racing on a track.

Raphael Akinrinade (9)
St Joseph's Primary School, London

Playground

I am standing in the freezing cold,
I can hear my friends laughing at jokes that are so boring.
I can hear the other kids shouting, 'Goal!'
I can hear the lashing of the skipping ropes as they hit the floor
Like a dog's tail.

I can hear the ball as it bounces back off the fence
I can hear a girl crying as she sits in the corner
I can hear the headmaster telling someone off
Like a mad buffalo charging at a little boy
I can hear the ding of the lunchtime bell.

I can see people chewing an apple
Fast like a leopard eating its prey
I can hear the birds singing
As they glide past like beautiful falcons
I can see teenagers arguing
As they walk past like stampeding elephants.
I can see my friends fighting over the ball
Like angry hyenas eating a deer.

I can see the mums,
I think it's time to go home.

Connor Leahy (8)
St Joseph's Primary School, London

Never Chew Gum In Class

My teacher is the best
In the west
Until I got gum in her hair,
I knew I should not chew gum in class.
But I could not last
A day without my gum,
First she gave me detention.
Because she had to cut her hair,
But it wasn't really my fault so . . .
She forgave me.

M'Balu Bangura (9)
St Joseph's Primary School, London

My Best Friend K'Shayne

My friend K'Shayne has a sweet caring voice
Like a nurse who cheers you up when you are feeling ill.

My friend K'Shayne smells as sweet as popcorn
That is covered in sugar.

My friend K'Shayne wears a rough blazer
As rough as sandpaper.

My friend K'Shayne and I will never break up
We will stick together like glue on paper.

My friend K'Shayne is sweet as a red rose
With a butterfly resting on the top

My friend K'Shayne is not just my friend
She is my best friend in the whole, wide world!

Natasha Ghandour (8)
St Joseph's Primary School, London

Friends' Feelings

My friends are sitting in the classroom
And I can smell my friends' perfume,
It is as fresh as washing-up liquid,
Drifting from her hair.
Sometimes, just to show off,
They bring in little bottles and spray them everywhere.

My friends are happy, they sing and dance,
They make one up every week!
I can see them dancing
They dance like springs going up and down.

Sometimes we have fallouts,
But we don't care because we are
Best friends.

Ellie McHugh (8)
St Joseph's Primary School, London

Football

Standing on the football pitch
In the middle of a game.
I see players kicking balls,
Like fireworks blasting off into space.

The players running like leaping leopards,
Trying to catch an antelope.

Footballs firing past,
Like cannonballs with flames of fire.

I hear the fans shouting,
Like roaring lions calling to their pack.

Suddenly a player fouls another,
Like a fierce rhino fighting in the African desert.

Ramiro Gonzalez Diaz (8)
St Joseph's Primary School, London

My Pet

Big and strong,
A bit dumb,
Like Dick and Dom
And a never-ending rumbling tum.

Ten years old,
Sharp claws,
Never gets cold,
Scratches floors.

When dinner's finished brewing,
With his sharp teeth,
He'll never stop chewing,
His very juicy beef.

George Marino (10)
St Joseph's Primary School, London

Tick-Tock, Tick-Tock

Tick-tock, tick-tock
I am hungry
Where is all my food?
Tick-tock, tick-tock.

Tick-tock, tick-tock
My belly is rebelling
Where are all my friends?
Tick-tock, tick-tock.

Tick-tock, tick-tock
My friend is hungry
Where is my packed lunch?
Tick-tock, tick-tock.

Tick-tock, tick-tock,
Where is my plate?
I think it is in the garbage
Tick-tock, tick-tock.

Juan Pino-Riano (8)
St Joseph's Primary School, London

My Teachers

Sitting down in my class
Listening to my teacher,
Talking like a dictionary,
Using words to help the children understand.

Watching my teacher,
Walking around on duty,
Looking after the children,
Like a lion protecting her cub.

She looks around the playground
And talks to the children
Chatting like birds in the trees.

Kiefer St-Louis (8)
St Joseph's Primary School, London

In The Sun

When it's sunny
Girls are playing with a skipping rope
Boys are playing basketball.

Everybody talking at once
Chat, chat.

When it's sunny
Boys play in the toilets shouting, 'Argh!'
Girls screaming, 'Argh!'

When it's sunny
Boys are chasing girls
Girls are screaming, 'Argh!'

When it's sunny
The boys and the girls are playing together.

Shannon Fullwood (7)
St Joseph's Primary School, London

Poem About Teachers

Teachers teaching their class,
Some are reading,
Some are talking,
Some are helping their class.

Teachers photocopying work for the children,
But the photocopier is broken,
Teachers are cross.

Teachers in the staffroom,
Teachers eating their lunch,
But one of the teachers has forgotten their lunch,
So the teacher didn't have anything.

Teacher's taking her class to lunch,
One of the children saying,
'I'm hungry.'

Holly Johnson (7)
St Joseph's Primary School, London

Sweet Mother

I love you, sweet Mother,
When I'm sick you make me well,
If I reveal my secrets, you will never tell,
You buy me all those stylish clothes,
When I have the sniffles, you wipe my nose.

I love you, sweet Mother,
When I'm down you make me smile,
You clean me as if I'm a dirt pile,
You love to help me with my work,
You also scare me so I jerk.

I love you, sweet Mother,
When I'm hungry you feed me,
You love to make me cups of tea,
When I'm with you I feel protected,
Because I know I won't be rejected
    By you, my sweet mother!

Ifeoma Abuka-Ahima (10)
St Joseph's Primary School, London

Working In School

Working at my table
Getting all my maths done
Lots of pencils breaking, sounding
Like snapping plastic
Everybody saying 'I'm finished.'

The bell has gone, we're having playtime,
Miss is sitting in the classroom
Marking all our work.

Connie Pembroke (8)
St Joseph's Primary School, London

Lunchtime

At lunchtime my tummy rumbles
Like a big, roaring bear in the dinner hall
I hear teachers telling off children,
'Stop talking.'

I hear children munching and crunching their food
I see children sitting nicely, getting ready to go out
In the playground I hear teachers
We play happily until we hear *ring*
The bell goes, time for class
Get into your lines, time to go.

Back in class it is time to do poetry work
And use our school laptops.

Antonia Krupa (7)
St Joseph's Primary School, London

Football

I can feel the blood dripping down my cheek
Like a raging waterfall,
I can see the goalkeeper diving with courage,
To catch the ball like a monkey,
When I am playing football I try my best to win.

I can see the goalkeeper kicking the ball out
Like an angry lion
I can see the air lifting the ball up high in the sky,
Like a balloon floating to the clouds.
I can hear kids shouting at other kids,
Like crazy monkeys having a fight.
When I am playing football I feel I am winning.

Charlotte Wallace (8)
St Joseph's Primary School, London

Playground

I am on my own
Standing in the corner of the playground.
I see boys playing football
And I see girls skipping nicely.
I see the teacher on duty drinking tea,
Looking at children playing nicely.
I see the head teacher through his window.
Boys are also playing football.
I see the boys stop playing football
And the girls begin a fight.
I see them fight and I begin to laugh.
I call the teacher to stop the fight.
Mr Eddie stopped the fight.

Romay Efrem (7)
St Joseph's Primary School, London

The Classroom

We're in the classroom
What do you see?
I see my teacher looking at me.

Teacher, teacher, what do you see?
Children talking 'n' thinking work is easy.

Children, children, what do you see?
It's nearly playtime, whoo, hee, hee, hee.

I'm outside, what do I see?
People playing football, that's fun to me!

We're inside, children what do you see?
Mr Macauley!

Raficia Rollings (8)
St Joseph's Primary School, London

Peace

Peace and harmony is what we need,
'Guns and knives put down,' I plead.
For all I know, for all I say,
Violence and cruelty is not the way.
Play with each other, be kind,
Because all we want is peace of mind.
So bring in the peace, put out the crime,
Do yourself a favour and do it in time.
There would be a better world without any riots,
It would be so peaceful, so quiet.
So as I send you to sleep,
Quietly creep,
With your teddy bear, Sheep,
Dream yourself away in the kingdom of peace.

Danielle Alexander (10)
St Joseph's Primary School, London

Love

She comforts when I'm in need,
She makes me secure when I cuddle her.
When I'm angry she makes me feel loved,
When I'm feeling down she's always there to pick up the pieces.
If I need someone to talk to, she's always there.

When I'm feeling sick she doesn't go to work,
Sometimes we have our differences, but she always comes back.
If I need any kind of protection, she treats me like a baby,
She brings a smile to my face.
She offers me the world whenever I need protection,
Whether I'm right or wrong.

Isabelle Hammond-Caines (10)
St Joseph's Primary School, London

Untitled

Brown fur around its body
My pet is my favourite hobby
Run around in spring
While I beautifully sing.

In the daytime you smile
But in a little while
You give me a hug
Then you sleep on your rug.

I look after you
Like a lion looks after its cubs
I feel you
Like a birds takes worms to its nest
I take you to bed
Like a cat takes its kittens to bed.

You're my best friend, rabbit.

Omoze Edeki (10)
St Joseph's Primary School, London

Homeless

Lonely in the world
Wishing you had a different life
Longing for someone to hold you
For someone to keep you safe
Hating yourself
Beating yourself up
Alone
Searching for a family
Waiting to be loved
To be owned
Crying out for help
Hoping somebody will listen
Left alone in darkness
In darkness once again.

Osezele Ilenbs (10)
St Joseph's Primary School, London

School

I like school
I like school, I think it is great
My mum drops me off at the gates
I run to meet all of my mates.

I really like school, I think it's cool
We learn things every day
And enjoy the times we get to play.

I'm a really wobbly writer
I need to hold my pen tighter
I need to be a lot neater
Says my neighbour, Peter.

The day ends, we go home
I've had a really great day
My mum picks me up from the gates
And I say goodbye to my mates.

Georgia Carter (8)
St Joseph's Primary School, London

Miss Emma

Miss Emma, Miss Emma,
When is it lunchtime, I can't wait to munch?

Miss Emma, Miss Emma,
When is it home time I can't wait to play with my baby cousin?

Miss Emma, Miss Emma,
When is it playtime I can't wait to play football?

Miss Emma, Miss Emma,
Is it time to go now?
I'm tired now and I want to go home.

Sophie Arnold (7)
St Joseph's Primary School, London

Lunchtime

Tick-tock,
'Teacher, is it lunchtime?'
'No,' said Miss Canden,
'Get on with your work.'

Tick-tock,
'Teacher, is it playtime?'
'Just get on with your maths.'

Tick-tock,
'Teacher, is it maths?'
'Just get on with your art.'

Tick-tock,
'Teacher, is it home time?'
'Just get on with your literacy.'

James Pembroke (7)
St Joseph's Primary School, London

On The Football Pitch

In the playground
There are some girls playing hopscotch
And boys playing football.

In the dinner hall
There is food everywhere
And drinks spilled on the floor.

In the classroom corner
There are lots of things to do
Like reading and playing with cards.

On the football pitch
There are puddles everywhere
Footballs fly and children shout.

George Rampling (7)
St Joseph's Primary School, London

Playtime

Thank God it's playtime,
I need some fun.
The teachers are driving me crazy,
I think I need some sunshine,
I'm feeling a little lazy.

They're playing there,
Now I'm here,
Somebody hurts their knee,
No who is he?
Oh yes, it's Charlie!

Oh no, Charlie gets me!
Now who should I get?
Ruby or Debbie or Reggie?
Back into class!

Louise O'Brien (7)
St Joseph's Primary School, London

Lunchtime

Tick-tock, what's the time?
Twelve o'clock for dinner time.

We all line up at the door,
Oops, I fell on the floor.

Off we go down the stairs,
To eat our lunch, munch, munch.

I've finished my lunch, I'm going out to play,
I'm having fun but today is the only day.

Now it is the end of the day
And it is time to go home.

Terri Duffin (7)
St Joseph's Primary School, London

The Playground

In the playground I stand on my own,
I see girls doing each other's hair.
Then I see boys playing football
And a teacher drinking coffee.

In the playground corner I stand alone,
I see big kids bullying little kids,
Girls skipping with ropes
And boys playing baseball.

In the playground corner I stand and see
A teacher, looking around.
The bell rings,
Girls doing clapping games
And everyone goes in.
Hey you, leave that kid alone!

Shinnelle Frimpong (8)
St Joseph's Primary School, London

Playground

We go to school,
We play with our friends,
We have the best time of our lives,
Then the whistle goes,
Play is over.

We go and do our maths,
'Don't talk Louise, please,
And Mollie Moo, I am watching you.'
Now it's time to go home.
When we go home,
We have got homework to do.
We say our goodbyes.
See you all tomorrow!

Ellie Marsters (7)
St Joseph's Primary School, London

The Desert

See all the crystal-brown sand,
Turned into mountains crawling up and up.
The taste of chicken drummers boiling hot,
Making your mouth water.
See the people swelter, grill and burn,
The sweat dripping off their heads.
Hot potatoes everywhere, burning people's feet.
When I see this, I think of crystal-brown gold
All over the floor and on the mountains.
It reminds me of a hot and warm sound.

Harry Glover (9)
St Joseph's Primary School, London

Cupid's Love Arrows

Cupid's bow and arrows are as red as lipstick,
They sound like crunching cherries,
They taste like strawberry ice cream,
The smell like rose oil and burning wood,
They look like the sweetness of sugar,
They feel like a load of fluffy, white, feathery pillows,
They remind me of sun-kissed roses, swaying swiftly and softly.

Jack Murphy (9)
St Joseph's Primary School, London

Arctic

'Tis platinum, like the clouds above me in the clear blue sky,
The penetrating taste of frozen ice will blow you away,
The howling of the wind will deafen you,
The Arctic looks like a blanket of snow,
The bitter freeze will spare no thought for anyone,
The Arctic reminds me of barren wasteland.

Rebecca Tobin (10)
St Joseph's Primary School, London

Lunchtime, Lunchtime

Lunchtime, lunchtime,
What shall I eat?
Oh wow, look at that jolly treat!

Lunchtime, lunchtime,
I know I hate beans,
I think I'll treat myself to a nice bowl of greens!

Lunchtime, lunchtime,
What a great lunch,
Who made that sound go *munch*?

Lunchtime, lunchtime,
Look at them eat,
I only have a piece of meat!

Lunchtime, lunchtime,
What a big bun,
I've got to get ready to have some fun!

Lunchtime, lunchtime,
Oh, I feel ill,
Would someone please get me a pill!

Lunchtime, lunchtime,
Run, please run,
Before you throw up on your plate!

Lunchtime, lunchtime,
It's beans on toast?
I would prefer Sunday roast!

Daniel Lawson (7)
St Joseph's Primary School, London

I Stand And See

I stand and see
A girl as little as a book
A pen as narrow as a road
A white board as big as an elephant.

I stand and see
A dolphin as big as a whale
A pencil case as thick as pastry
A dog as thick as an engine
A bulb as hot as fire.

I stand and see
A hat as short as a zip
A lever as hard as a wall
A brick as steely as a railing
A saddle as soft as leather.

I stand and see
Water pouring like a waterfall
A book bag as flat as pastry
A T-shirt as wide as the streets
A box as empty as a pot.

I stand and see
A car driving as quickly as a motorbike
A fire engine sordid like a whale
A lid squashed like a piece of metal
An elastic band stretched like Blu-tack.

I stand and see
A teacher as tall as a giraffe
A paper soft as cotton wool
A pencil as small as a tadpole.

Peter Vu (7)
St Joseph's Primary School, London

Counting Carry Boxes

Ten carry boxes in the class
All sitting happily
Then lots of children run so fast
One goes, so there are nine.

Nine carry boxes playing in the park
All the lights go out
Now it is dark
One goes, so there are eight.

Eight carry boxes lying on a bed
Just about to fall asleep
When they see Father Ted
One goes, so there are seven.

Seven carry boxes having a bite
Some turn round
What a sight
One goes, so there are six.

Six carry boxes talking to a mate
Sinning and laughing
Some reckon they're late
One goes, now there are five.

Five cute carry boxes sitting on a mat
Bickering and bouncing
Oh no, here comes the cat
One goes, so there are four.

Four clever carry boxes playing lots of tricks
They look up
And see falling bricks
One goes, now there are three.

Three colourful carry boxes sitting on a bench
They bend down and get drenched
One goes, now there are two.

Two carry boxes jumping up and down
They stop jumping
And see a frown
One goes, now there is one.

Ruby Dempsey (7)
St Joseph's Primary School, London

Hate

'Tis the colour of black after charcoal burning.
The sound of goblins cackling, leaves a provoking feeling.
A bitter lemon dripping on my tongue, making me crunch.
After the Devil's ten-mile run, the stench travels through my nose.
The sight of a good Samaritan falling into Hell makes me
                                        exasperated.
The universe tumbling upside down, makes me feel depressed.
Sadness reminds me truly.

Blessing Bakare (10)
St Joseph's Primary School, London

The Jungle

The colour of the jungle is green, like vegetables.
A jungle sounds like a hunter ambushed it.
The jungle tastes like a strong stalk of broccoli
And crispy leaves like a tree swaying in the breeze.
The jungle smells like bright, fresh plants growing from their roots,
Like worms going down into the ground.
The jungle looks like a palm tree digging into me.
The jungle feels like knobbly jellyfish, like cannonballs blasting out.
The jungle reminds me of animals roaming around.

Jacob Spooner (10)
St Joseph's Primary School, London

Friendship

My friend is always there for me,
She never lets me down,
My friend is caring,
She's always a funny clown.

She's never shy to admit what's wrong,
She's a generous, reliable friend,
My friend is the one that's good for me,
I know that this is right.

She gives me a petal,
She buys me a daisy
And she's the kindest friend of all.

We talk about boys,
We share our secrets,
Hugs and kisses we share together.

Gloria Titilayo (10)
St Joseph's Primary School, London

Deserts

Deserts are yellow,
Like the sun has washed the surface
Since it first came out.
They smell of the sun,
Beating down on the camels
And making them sweat.
They taste of crunchy lemons
Which are extremely hot.
They sound like the sun beating on the sand.
They look like sand piled on the whole land.
They feel like tawny coloured flowers
Getting poured into a bowl.
Deserts remind me of the sunrise,
Coming up from the ground.

Jamie Hayden (9)
St Joseph's Primary School, London

The Desert

Like appetizing, sweet tangerines coloured bright orange,
Lions roaring as the sandstorms blow is the lonely sound,
Stale bread is the taste as it is so moistureless,
The scent is fresh air hovering all around you,
The gathering of sand going on forever are its interesting looks,
A furnace of fire spreading across the land
Blocks out all other feelings,
An abandoned land, the relentless wind
Constantly shifting and changing its shape.

Casey Sullivan (10)
St Joseph's Primary School, London

Rainforest

Rainforest is so green, like pretty, new, growing grass.
A sound in the rainforest is like rain falling
Unhurriedly on the ground, *pitter-patter, pitter-patter.*
The taste is like sweet honey from the centre of a beehive.
In my hand all soft and gentle, I feel a leaf rubbing against my hand.
You can hear the sweet birds singing after they wake from
their slumber.

Sophie Warner (10)
St Joseph's Primary School, London

The Beach

It's bright, like the sun blasting down on my neck,
A rushing sound of a stampede of Indian elephants,
The taste of a big, juicy watermelon running down my tongue,
The smell of the delicious salted fish and chips in my beautiful
banana bowl,
The sun goddess burning her fury on the little, beautiful beach,
It reminds me of the first time I went to Pontins.

Yannick Edmond (11)
St Joseph's Primary School, London

Classroom

Multicoloured, like a glittering rainbow,
Sounds like a procession of roaring lions waiting anxiously
for their supper,
Try resisting the taste, as delicious ham sandwiches' smell
fills the air,
The smell of the fashionable school dinners ready to be munched,
travels round this place.
It looks crowded with sets of colours, every colour of the rainbow
is there,
You feel all stuffy, like a mass of pillows and feathers are
surrounding you,
However, this place reminds you of a jungle, swarming with all
sorts of animals, in assembly.

Alexa Alarcon-Mensah (9)
St Joseph's Primary School, London

Flowers

I see flowers standing tall like soldiers.
Flowers smell like a sweet apple shining in the sun.
My flowers look like a herd of buffalo shimmering in the hot sun.
Flowers feel like a seal's fur coat.
A flower tastes like jam.
A flower sounds like rustling from the fruit in the trees.

George Arnold (10)
St Joseph's Primary School, London

Garden

I can hear the birds singing through the rustic trees,
I can taste the fresh air as it tickles my throat,
I can smell perfume bursting from flowers,
It looks like a peaceful, calm garden and gives me the feeling of love,
This reminds me of a kiss that's just blown.

Charlotte Ewing (9)
St Joseph's Primary School, London

Heaven

A pleasant place where birds sing beautiful songs,
Leaves me with a sweet feeling in my joyful heart.
Candyfloss leaves a fabulous taste in my mouth,
Reminding me of the time I visited the fair.
Heaven smells like a beauty shop
With perfume spreading everywhere.
This peaceful place looks like a town of marvellous angels
Playing their harps.
This fantastic place feels like a field of heavenly people
Praising the Lord.
This sensible placed feels like a warm feeling from my heart,
Spreading love.
Heaven reminds me of my family,
Because when we are all together, we all have a laugh.

Daniel Igbinedion (9)
St Joseph's Primary School, London

Rainforests

The sound of a roaring, distant river gushing downhill,
Fills my ears.
An exotic fruit salad, makes my taste buds
Tingle teasingly.
The temperature is like a jack-in-the-box
And plays unforgiving tricks on everybody's feelings.
Even while day, the massive, high canopy
Prevents the sun's rays from penetrating to the ground
And casts the space beneath in an everlasting twilight,
The tall trees lined up like soldiers,
Their enormous helmets blocking out the sun.

Charlie Beales (9)
St Joseph's Primary School, London

Desert

The desert sounds like a slithering snake.
The desert tastes like the sweet coconut.
It smells like snake's skin.
The desert looks like a bunch of snakes crawling up to you.
The desert feels like a trapped up place.
It reminds me of a city getting flooded.

Daniel Cerullo (9)
St Joseph's Primary School, London

Heaven

Delightful, sweet children filled with happiness.
As I devour sweet peaches and cream,
The taste fills me with delight and contentment.
There in Heaven, I can smell the fragrance of beautiful lilies.
To me, Heaven feels like a loving and caring place.
Heaven is a place where all your dreams come true.
Heaven reminds me of true love.

Yvette Ndede (9)
St Joseph's Primary School, London

Desert

The desert sounds like a camel is approaching me,
Kicking the sand.
It tastes like the salty sea.
It smells like wet sand.
The desert looks like a small, deserted, sandy place.
The sand feels soft, dry and smooth.
The desert reminds me of a seaside without water.

Katie Corbett (9)
St Joseph's Primary School, London

Sports Day

You can win,
You can lose,
There are lots of races
To choose.

You can jump,
You can have fun,
But the best thing to do
Is to run.

Listen carefully to instructions,
Then you will see,
You can be a sports day winner,
Just like me.

My friends filled me with delight,
When I won the matches,
I was filled with gold, bright happiness
And I got all my catches.

I fell down over my lace
And I was unhappy,
Because I lost the race.
I nearly won them,
But I lost one of my matches,
It's because they lost their catches.

Ayomide Idowu (7)
St Joseph's Primary School, London

Rainforest

Green, like fresh cut grass on a summer morning.
The sound of hundreds of mice squeaking at the heavy rain.
It smells salty, like the Dead Sea.
Infinite shades of green hit you wherever you go.
Reminds me of the first time spent night-walking in the forest.

Jack Kelly (10)
St Joseph's Primary School, London

The Arctic

Dreaming of a bright, warm, sunny morning,
Like a sunrise appearing over the horizon.

A powerful, swirling wind,
Reminds me of the sound of lions roaring for meat.

Drinking my freezing glass of Coke,
I can smell the sweet fragrance of vanilla.

A melting icicle that is frozen from the bitter cold,
It reminds me of a white, snowy Christmas.

Natalie Montes (10)
St Joseph's Primary School, London

Friendship

Someone to share all my feelings with,
To go shopping, cinema or somewhere new.
Enjoy a cosy sleepover,
Cheers me up when I'm feeling sad.
To play make-believe football and dance,
To talk about clothes and fashion with.
Makes me laugh when I'm feeling mad,
What a great thing to have.

Elise Fairbairn (10)
St Joseph's Primary School, London

Rainforest

It tastes like all the tropical animals calling for help,
But it tastes like all the tropical fruit hanging from the trees.
The beautiful aroma of a crispy leaf.
It looks like the rainfall crashing on the open, wild rocks.
On the other hand, it feels like the summer breeze blowing
                                                on my face.
So it reminds me of a little island called Mauritius.

Joshua Akif (9)
St Joseph's Primary School, London

My Brother

Friendship giver
Joy bringer
Food muncher
Drink slurper
Gel user
Telly watcher
Computer player
Room messer
Dirt putter
Girl lover
Club ruler
Gym visitor
Karate worker
Black belter
Kitchen explorer
Hair spiker
My brother.

Simona Castagno (11)
St Joseph's Primary School, London

Football

Playing the game,
Can be nervous,
It also brings pain,
But watching it is always anxious.

Being beaten is such sadness,
But when victorious,
I fill with happiness,
Just like scoring a goal.

The roar of the crowd like lions at the zoo,
When I am on the ball, brings much delight,
But when I get tackled, it's disappointing,
To not see that beautiful goal.

Scott Watson (10)
St Joseph's Primary School, London

Love

Henri is my friend
He offers me unconditional love
I think about him all the time
When I feel sad, he makes me happy.

Henri sometimes growls at me
We compete for my mum's attention
And when he sleeps, he snores too loud
His kisses are too smelly to mention.

Henri is always on my mind
We go to the park together
He chases my ball for hours
Most of all, he's very loyal.

I'm never alone with Henry by my side
Lying together eating his bone.

Rebecca Webb (10)
St Joseph's Primary School, London

Friendship

My friend brings a smile to my face
When I need someone she is there
If I'm in need of protection, I give her a call
When I feel lonely she is there.

We share happy times together
When I have a problem she is there
We go to the park, we go out shopping
When I'm in need of a hug she is there.

We've spent many years at school together
When I'm feeling left alone she is there
We talk together and share our feelings
When I need her help she is there.

Mary Kpagoi (10)
St Joseph's Primary School, London

Sports Day

Sports day, sports day,
Running all around,
Sports day, sports day,
No falling on the ground.

Sports day, sports day,
Is fun for everyone,
Sports day, sports day,
Our medals weigh a ton.

Sports day, sports day,
Our faces bright red,
Sports day, sports day,
We're ready for bed.

Sports day, sports day,
Where's my ted?
Sports day, sports day,
It's bedtime for me.

Lauren Davis (7)
St Joseph's Primary School, London

Love

Love is the sunlight that shines in my eyes
It's something that brings me joy
Love never makes anyone cry
It brings people happiness
Just like a child and a toy.
Love is always creative
It's hard to find or see
And is never destructive
Love always puts a smile on my face.

Oluwagbeminiyi Tinubu (10)
St Joseph's Primary School, London

My Cat

Mouse snatcher
Fish catcher
Chicken killer
Fox fighter
Energy radiator
Tree climber
Door opener
Table jumper
Chair scratcher
Meat lover
Stroke liker
Child rubber
Dog hater
Rabbit muncher
Curtain destroyer

Is a loyal and trusting friend,
Would stick by me until the end.
He has claws as sharp as knives,
Some might say he has nine lives.

He balances with a furry tail,
Nobody could ever say he's frail.
He runs around, happy and free,
But always he comes back to me.

Catches mice with great delight,
He could win in any fight!
So from the beginning, until the end,
He'll always be my favourite friend!

Barney Holleran (10)
St Joseph's Primary School, London

Cat

Cute, furry, little creature
She has big, staring eyes
Her little pink nose is her main feature
She falls off the table and cries
She would bow to Jesus Christ.

Crunch, crunch, goes her food
When she's eating in the kitchen
She runs around when she's in a good mood
She also ran after a pigeon
She is the best cat in the world!

Food robber
Insect masher
Furniture destroyer
China crasher
Mouse catcher
Couch ripper
Guest scratcher
Wasp killer
Ball chaser.

Andrej Libakov-Livanov (10)
St Joseph's Primary School, London

Family

F amilies are always gathered
A nd will always love you.
M ore love is in their hearts for you.
I s going to support you always.
L oves you.
Y ou are special to them.

Shamick Edmond (11)
St Joseph's Primary School, London

Materials

Glass for my marbles, which roll and shine,
Wood for my chair, when I sit in line.
A plastic flask for my lunchtime drink,
Shiny metal on the taps in the sink.
Pretty pottery pots with flowers in,
If they break on the floor, they make a din.

Materials, materials everywhere,
With lots of uses for us to share.

Alex Tunstall (7)
St Mark's Primary School, Hanwell

The Magic Box
(Based on 'Magic Box' by Kit Wright)

I will put in the box . . .
A feather of a sonic bird faster than the wind,
A mad bull attacking a horse and then eating it up,
A flying carpet flying like a plane,
A giant meteor coming from space,
A polar climate where a cold snowman will be.

Daniel Olweny
St Mark's Primary School, Hanwell

The Sea

Quiet sea with nobody there and I am looking out to sea,
Picking up shells as I look at the sea.
Go past me.
As I pick shells up, a seagull comes to see me,
Lots of them, lots of them coming for me.
They are scaring me, *argh!*

Acen Oduka
St Mark's Primary School, Hanwell

The Sea

You go to the beach in summer,
You go to the beach in winter.
Fishermen catching fish for their tea,
Wind blowing in their hair.
When I walk, the sand crunches under my feet.
Tiny fish getting chased by a barracuda.
The cliffs are very dangerous because they are high.
Look! A beached jellyfish,
But don't touch it, they can sting you.
But now the ice cream shop is closed,
It is time to go home.

Tomos Tabern (8)
St Mark's Primary School, Hanwell

The Alien In The Spaceship

In space there was an alien playing games,
He was very unhappy because people kept calling him names.
He got out of the spaceship and he got on a plane,
He went to England and never went back to space again.
In England he met a friend called Shane,
Shane was a boy who lived down the lane.
His sister was insane
And his uncle was chained up in chains.

Shane Waugh (8)
St Mark's Primary School, Hanwell

Wind

The wind blows like an owl howling and screaming,
Brushing past your face.
It feels so gentle, but so cool.
At night you can hear the wind's mighty powers,
Flowing through the air and brushing against the trees.

Archie Pearson (7)
St Mark's Primary School, Hanwell

The Hedgehog

There was a little hedgehog,
Who looked just like a dog.

He kept his house very neat,
But he had very big feet.

He went to his tiny house
And caught a big, fat, old mouse.

Then he went to bed all nice,
With a feeling of all those fat mice.

Thomas Langford (9)
St Mark's Primary School, Hanwell

The Secret

Secrets in the corner, secrets everywhere,
How do you know if a secret's there if you do not look?
If you tell a secret, you must beware that no one is there,
They will find out your secret if you are not careful.
Secrets in the corner, secrets in a box,
If you love secrets, then listen to this,
Secrets in the corner, secrets in a box,
If you love secrets, then this poem is for you.

Amy Ferguson (8)
St Mark's Primary School, Hanwell

People

People are coming to town
Seagulls flying around
Me sleeping in my comfy bed
Mum writing in her notepad
Dad snoring, fast asleep
My sister having lovely dreams
And last, my cat purring in her basket.

Morgan Chauvin (8)
St Mark's Primary School, Hanwell

Fireworks

F lames are glowing
I ncredible fireworks are going
R ockets spinning, sparkles sprinkling
E verybody, fireworks are twinkling
W onderful fireworks over my head
O h, how will I ever get to bed?
R oaring and whistling all night long
K ing rockets, please don't go wrong
S o everybody, have a good time on fireworks night!

Nia Tabern (9)
St Mark's Primary School, Hanwell

Dinner Monster

One evening when I cracked my egg,
A monster jumped out with a hairy head.
I'm telling you straight (and it ain't no joke),
He was standing there all covered in yolk.

When he stared at me he was full of laughter,
Then he washed himself in my glass of water.
He dried himself on the Evening Post,
Then helped himself to my piece of toast.

Mark Jones (9)
St Mark's Primary School, Hanwell

The Sea

The fishes swimming in the Pacific Ocean,
Swimming swiftly with me.
Seagulls flying on top of me.
There are crabs on the shore, *click, click!*
Mum and me surf on the sea.
My dad watches me.
Seagulls flying to cliffs.

Oliver Jones (8)
St Mark's Primary School, Hanwell

The Crazy Lion

There is a lion that I know
Who stands on his nose and calls himself a crow.
He never stops dressing up and acting silly
And when he does, he calls himself Billy.
He calls me names, but I do the same,
He never plays my games.
He's just always mucking around
And rolling on the ground.
But sometimes he's a bit funny,
Pretending to be Mr Bunny.
Doing maths and doing science,
But by the end of the playing day,
He doesn't want to play,
He just wants to snuggle in bed,
Without bumping his head
And waiting for tomorrow,
Hoping to do more crazy things
And as you can see, just like me,
He is a crazy lion.

Sonny Poon-Tip (8)
St Mark's Primary School, Hanwell

The Swan

Swimming silently across the icy river,
The swan.
Moonlight shining, trees swaying,
All leaves gone.
Middle of winter, snowstorms coming,
Slowly flapping her silver wings
The moon is watching,
Glowing rings around the stars.
Of all of the birds, she is the best,
The river's rushes are her rest.

Elinor Percival (9)
St Mark's Primary School, Hanwell

Wildlife

I saw a bear trying to catch some fish,
Then eating them on its bloodstained dish.
I saw it again in a cage at the fair
And that's the last time I saw the young bear.
After that I saw a beautiful deer
And as it stood still, I got really near.
Suddenly the deer ran into the woods,
I heard a *bang* and understood,
The deer had been shot for hunter food.
I'd rather be in a lion's tum,
Then ask the hunters what they'd done.
But that's exactly what I did,
They said they'd killed it for their kid.
I told Dad that they'd shot the deer
And that I'd run away in fear.
My father didn't believe me though,
I said to him, 'I want to go.'
I asked him, 'When we get home can we have bread?'
He said, 'But I was going to make deer.'
I screamed.

Jack Barry (8)
St Mark's Primary School, Hanwell

My Hamster, Harold

Harold is my hamster and he is very fat
He is so fat, he looks like a cat
Harold is my hamster, he is very greedy
He likes to have a massage because he's very needy
Harold is my hamster, he is grey and black
He has a special cage that looks just like a shack
Harold is my hamster, he likes to waddle along
He is always trying to escape and then he was gone
Harold is my hamster, we found him under the stair
I was so pleased to see him, I gave him a little pear.

Georgina Jefferson (9)
St Mark's Primary School, Hanwell

Super Dog

There is a dog who has super powers,
He flies around for absolute hours.
He fought crime,
But now he's mine and this is how it happened.

I found him one day
And there he lay,
He'd been shot by crime,
So I made him mine.

His age is ten
And his name is Ben.
His favourite food is sausage and chips
And there's always sauce around his lips.

Daniel Beaumont (9)
St Mark's Primary School, Hanwell

May I Play?

Every day I sit and wait
For the children to come out to play.
There are girls and boys
With skipping ropes and lots of toys.

They shout and run,
Play and laugh,
Chase each other
And have so much fun.

I so very much want to join in,
I follow them around and around and call and call.
Sadly, I do not seem to be heard,
I suppose that's because I am just a little bird.

Abigail Richards (9)
St Mark's Primary School, Hanwell

Teachers

Strict, strict, strict,
Nag, nag, nag,
Moaning teachers all day long,
Telling people to get on.

Miles Purchese (10)
St Mary's RC School, Barnard Castle

My Grandma

She always bakes me a cake
And she walks as fast as a leopard.
She always sits smartly,
With her arms folded in front of her.
Her cakes are scrumptious,
She always makes me butterfly cakes.
She always gets me sweets.
Every word she says is polite.
I love my grandma,
She's the best in the world.
She always makes me laugh at night!
My grandma's face is square,
Her mouth is big and her hands are fat.

Katie Thompson (9)
Stanton Middle School, Bradville

My Sea Poem

Sea is as an ocean
Waves ripple as fast as an eagle
Sea horses bob up and down above the waves
Sharks patrol in the deep
Oceans still to be revealed.

Danielle Gibbons (9)
Stow Heath Junior School, Portobello

Flowers

Prettily blooming in the scorching heat,
Daisies, buttercups and daffodils laze at my feet.
Decorating and putting in a superior smell
And then falling when not watered well.

Red, orange, green and blue,
Looking at the colours will help make the day pass through.
Standing in diminutive and immense vases on the window sills
And then you can overlook the gigantic bills.

Fake or real, looking at them,
You will find out they are a gem.
They are pleasurable to have all day,
It doesn't matter if you have to pay.

Attractive leaves is what it boasts about
And if someone says that they look ugly, I do doubt.
If you don't know what these life-thrilling beauties are,
Then you are so behind, so far . . . *flowers!*

Tanya Rai (9)
Stow Heath Junior School, Portobello

Emotion Poem

Happiness looks like a bright yellow sun
Happiness tastes like biting into a sugary pancake
Happiness smells like fresh roses
Happiness is blue like the wavy sea
Happiness sounds like people cheering
Happiness feels like you have reached the top.

Sadness looks like a dull rainstorm
Sadness tastes cold and sour
Sadness smells like a damp, mouldy cloth
Sadness is black and grey like a rainstorm
Sadness sounds quiet
Sadness feels like you have no one.

Amy Whittingham (9)
Stow Heath Junior School, Portobello

My Emotion Poem

Happiness is like the sunset noon,
Happiness smells of sweet flowers,
Happiness tastes of strawberries and cream,
Happiness sounds like the breeze rushing through your hair,
Happiness feels like smooth velvet.

Sadness is like the black clouds in the sky,
Sadness smells of out of date milk,
Sadness tastes of sour apples,
Sadness sounds like people screaming and crying,
Sadness feels like rough surfaces.

Geeta Chumber (9)
Stow Heath Junior School, Portobello

All About Me

I run down the football field shouting,
'On my head.'
After a match I am really tired
And just want to go to bed.
Arsenal is my favourite team,
To play for them is my dream.
I watch them play and say,
'That will be me one day.'

Ryan Russell (8)
Stow Heath Junior School, Portobello

My Emotion Poem

Happiness is yellow like the sun
It tastes like banana ice cream
It looks like a bright light in the sky
It smells like a sunflower
It sounds like a flute playing
It feels like a warm feeling.

Danielle Campbell-Williams (9)
Stow Heath Junior School, Portobello

All About Me

Special, pretty,
I'm also witty!

Me, quite neat,
Really sweet!

Silent, cool,
Yes, I never act the fool!

When I'm bored I sing,
I'm worth a diamond ring!

Poetic, yes cute, leader of a ballet team,
The girl you'll see in your dreams.

Jodie Louza (8)
Stow Heath Junior School, Portobello

My Emotion Poem

Badness is red, like a red devil.
It tastes like rotten strawberries.
It smells like smelly, mouldy, disgusting milk.
It looks like brown dirt.
It sounds like a vase crashing to the floor.
It feels like being trapped.

Charlotte Macmanomy (9)
Stow Heath Junior School, Portobello

All About Me

I like school
Because they take us to the swimming pool.

They teach us how to swim,
Then we do PE in the gym.

We have to write stories and poems that rhyme,
It will take me 'til bedtime.

Rebecca Plant (8)
Stow Heath Junior School, Portobello

All About Me

Jodie May Highfield is the name I've got,
I like it a lot!

My teacher says I always smile and help out,
She never has to shout.

I never moan and groan,
Since Year 3 I have grown.

Now I am in Year 4,
I do even more!

Jodie Highfield (8)
Stow Heath Junior School, Portobello

All About Me

I like going to school,
Because it is very cool.

We always do lots of sport,
But I'm not very good because I'm short.

I'm always first in for dinner,
You might even say I'm the winner.

In lessons I think I'm the best,
But the teacher thinks I'm a pest.

Jamie Bowen (9)
Stow Heath Junior School, Portobello

My Emotion Poem

Sadness is black and grey, like a dark, spooky chimney.
It tastes like lumpy custard.
It smells like an old, dusty tower.
It looks dull and dark.
It sounds like anger and hatred.
It feels like I am alone.

Jaspreet Kaur Japper (9)
Stow Heath Junior School, Portobello

Animal Teachers

Just the other day,
Something got in my way.
I was sitting under the tree,
Along came Mr Bee,
Who took my tuck off me.

Mr Mole is a funny old soul,
But sometimes he makes you feel like jumping down a hole.
He shouts and sprays all over you
And so he makes you scream back too!

Miss Salmon is always asleep,
She scribbles and dribbles all over the desk,
Then at play she will say . . .
'Oi you, why have you done no work today?'

My favourite teacher I've got to say,
Is the one who lets us out at the end of the day!

Holly Taylor (10)
Stow Heath Junior School, Portobello

All About Me

Aidan Lewis is my name,
Wolves are down, what a shame,
(I support West Brom).

I like football,
Especially when we score.
West Brom are up and Wolves are below,
There is another match tomorrow.
They will hear me cheer,
Loud and clear.
The match is done
And we have won.

Aidan Lewis (8)
Stow Heath Junior School, Portobello

My Brothers

Kieran:

Kieran Lennard is so wicked
And has really cool mates.
He likes to hang around with them,
But comes home in awful states.

Kieran can be generous,
He sometimes can be kind,
But at the rate he's going,
I'll kick him up the behind!

Kyle:

Kyle Lennard is really cool
And he likes to bounce around,
He hugs his mum all the time,
He likes the echo sound.

Kyle normally is quite cute
And he always smiles,
But when it comes to animals,
He's scared of crocodiles - *arghh!*

Holly Lennard (10)
Stow Heath Junior School, Portobello

All About Me

I am 8 years old,
That's what I've been told.

I can run really quick,
And often play a trick.

My hair is spiky and fair,
Cool clothes I wear.

All this is true,
I can guarantee you.

Jake Cox (9)
Stow Heath Junior School, Portobello

All About Me

My teacher says I am quiet and good at school,
Because I listen to the rule.

I am tall and my hair is dark,
After school I play in the park.

My friend is the same as before,
We ask can we play some more.

I want to get my work right,
So I do homework at night.

Lauren Potts (8)
Stow Heath Junior School, Portobello

All About Me

Hello, I can act like a clown,
Everyone tells me to calm down!

I run around the house like a killer cat,
My sister's like a vampire bat.

I have a dream to rocket to the moon,
At the moment I only have a balloon!

'That won't take me sky-high,'
I mutter with a sigh.

Joseph James (8)
Stow Heath Junior School, Portobello

My Emotion Poem

Love is deep red, like a rose.
It tastes like a fresh strawberry.
It smells like nice floating air.
Love looks like two hearts joining.
Love sounds like two hearts happy.
It feels as if somebody has just been born.

Jamie Haynes (10)
Stow Heath Junior School, Portobello

All About Me

When I am at school,
I always act cool.

Five days a week,
I have to be quiet - not speak.

It is my place,
To sit in this space.

I have to read and write
And I hope I get it right.

Sasha Perry (8)
Stow Heath Junior School, Portobello

Feelings

Fear is as dark as night
Fear is a ghost just out of sight
Fear is a room without a light
Fear is never winning a fight.

Happiness is like the sun shining bright
Happiness is a warm bed late at night
Happiness is flying a colourful kite
Happiness is getting your homework right.

Heather Cockfield (10)
Stow Heath Junior School, Portobello

My Emotion Poem

Hate is red, like dark, bad blood.
It tastes of cold soup running on your tongue.
It smells of rotten apples still rotting in a fruit bowl.
It looks like a big, boiling hot person yelling in the street.
It sounds like people screaming and dogs fighting.
It feels like a too hot liquid running down your throat.
Hate!

Emily Callaghan (9)
Stow Heath Junior School, Portobello

All About Me

My favourite team is Arsenal
And I'm always wanting to open the parcel.

Everyone thinks I'm the best,
Whilst the teacher thinks I'm a pest.

Ravi is my name,
I have a wicked aim.

I have a creative folder,
Which I'll look at when I'm older.

I live in a big city,
I don't see much of it, which is a pity.

Highbury is the Arsenal ground
And it will be crowned.

Arsenal are the best
And they have beat the test.

Arsenal are a team
And they are the theme.

Arsenal were the champions last season
And they have reason.

Arsenal have a football shop
And have the best top.

I have an Arsenal towel
And they have never fouled.

Ravinder Gill (8)
Stow Heath Junior School, Portobello

Emotion Poem

Happiness:

Happiness is as pink as summer blossom,
It tastes like strawberry and cream sweets,
It smells like fresh air on a spring morning,
It sounds like a classical song,
It feels like fluffy kittens as they purr.

Sadness:

Sadness is as blue as the sea,
It tastes like lumpy mashed potato,
It smells as rotten as cabbage cooking,
It looks like a gloomy forest with nettles and bats,
It sounds like ghosts in a haunted house,
It feels like a spiky hedgehog.

Emy Brown (9)
Stow Heath Junior School, Portobello

Happiness

Happiness is a day when nothing goes wrong,
Like all the world is helping you stay strong,
And all the world joins hands and sings a jolly song.

Happiness is a feeling that makes you feel good,
When you don't know what to do, it tells you what you should
And when you feel there is nothing to do, it tells you what you could.

Happiness is a gift - given from your family and friends,
It shows your life is good when you wished your world would end
And when you feel your life has shattered, it will help it mend.

Max Sheffield (9)
Stow Heath Junior School, Portobello

My Emotion Poem

Sadness is a grey colour, like a stormy cloud,
It tastes like lukewarm soup running down your throat,
It smells like fresh flowers with no smell,
It looks like a deserted dog with no owner,
It sounds like people crying,
It feels like your heart turning to dust.

Happiness is as red as bright roses,
It tastes like the sweetest and loveliest apple pie,
It smells like fresh strawberries growing in a field,
It looks like people crying non-stop,
It sounds like screaming and bawling,
It feels like your heart turning to dust.

Rhianne Springthorpe (10)
Stow Heath Junior School, Portobello

All About Me

I just love yummy chocolate cake,
It normally gives me tummy ache.

Have you guessed that I am a girl?
I twist and dance and twirl.

I have a cat who is very fat,
She shouldn't be that!

My teacher says I have a lovely smile,
I think I'll sit here for quite a while!

I am making this poem rhyme,
But it does take a long time.

Sarah Whitehouse (8)
Stow Heath Junior School, Portobello

My Emotion Poem

Hate is the colour black,
It smells like a burnt chocolate cake,
Sounds like never-ending screams,
Looks like a dead rose,
It feels rough like a hard shell,
I hate the word hate!

Love is the colour red,
It smells like a fresh rose,
Sounds like laughter,
Looks like a bowl of strawberries,
It feels soft, like a silk pillow,
Tastes like sugar and spice and all things nice,
I love the word love.

Shannon Luck (10)
Stow Heath Junior School, Portobello

All About Me

Bex is my nickname,
To do well is my aim.

If I make a mistake,
More care I must take.

I like to paint and draw,
Especially now I am in Year 4.

I really try hard to be good,
I am glad that is understood.

Rebecca Robinson (8)
Stow Heath Junior School, Portobello

My Emotion Poem

Happiness is yellow, like the bright sun in the sky,
It tastes like fresh oranges all juicy and sweet,
It smells like the most expensive perfume you can get,
It looks like a field of pretty flowers,
It sounds like children playing on the beach,
It feels like being with a friend.

Sadness is grey, like the clouds when it's just rained,
It tastes like the salty blue sea,
It smells like rotten apples all battered and disgusting,
It looks like a messy room with things on the floor,
It sounds like screaming and yelling for help,
It feels like cold rooms when you get locked inside.

Stephanie Jones (9)
Stow Heath Junior School, Portobello

All About Me

Hi, my name is Sasha and I go to Stow Heath Junior School
And at this school I rule because I'm cool.

My teacher's name is Mrs Williams and she is very good,
She makes me do what I should.

When I am bored I love to dance
And my mom is trying very hard to find romance!

I have a pet hamster and his name is JJ
And he always sleeps in the day.

I have had to make new friends here,
I shall play with them through the year.

Sasha Cox (8)
Stow Heath Junior School, Portobello

My Emotion Poem

Sadness is black, like the night,
It tastes like poison,
It smells like cat litter,
It looks like an empty room,
It sounds silent,
It feels like your pet has died.

Happiness is yellow, like the sun,
It tastes like cakes,
It smells like fresh cut grass,
It looks like sparkling stars,
It sounds like coconuts banging together,
It feels like rabbits' fur.

Charlotte Howell (9)
Stow Heath Junior School, Portobello

Fear

Fear is a child only accompanied by air,
Fear is a nuclear bomb exploding without a care,
Fear is an excruciating pain,
Like a dagger through a vein,
Fear is having stage fright,
Fear is getting kidnapped at night,
Fear is an almighty cry,
Like you are about to die,
Fear is when you're about to lose,
A marvellous, beautiful holiday cruise.

Daniel Sowinski (10)
Stow Heath Junior School, Portobello

My Emotion Poem

Love is pink, like pretty pink flowers,
It tastes like fresh strawberry milkshake with lovely ice cream,
It smells of perfume from beautiful pink,
It looks like a big heart with lots of love,
It sounds like a street full of happy and loving people,
It feels like nothing could harm you.

Hate is dark red, like an evil red devil,
It tastes like a really hot, red heart,
It smells like a dead skeleton rusted for years,
It looks like a heart gone lonely with black tears,
It sounds like a street of children dead,
It feels like nothing.

Baljinder Sondh (10)
Stow Heath Junior School, Portobello

My Very Own Emotion Poem

Love is as gentle as a rose.
Love shoots up and down you and never stops.
Love tastes like berry pie.
Love feels like winter's breeze.
Love sounds like two birds singing.

Hate feels like hard metal.
Hate sounds like an old rickety car.
Hate is so nasty, like a knife.
Hate can kill you over a long time.

Glen Reece (9)
Stow Heath Junior School, Portobello

All About Me

My teacher says I talk a lot
And that I have to stop.

I have a lot to say,
Sometimes it takes all day!

What she doesn't know and see,
Is that it is just me!

I am the best at ping-pong,
Sometimes I take really long.

I want to be in Santa's sleigh,
But when I dream, I am eating hay.

Ethan Westwood (8)
Stow Heath Junior School, Portobello

All About Me

Call my name,
I'm always the one to blame.

Sit down, find a book,
Have a look.

I'll be in trouble yet,
You can bet.

'He tries,'
The teacher sighs.

Adam Cooke (8)
Stow Heath Junior School, Portobello

Giant, Giant

Giant, giant, where could you be?
Are you over here?
Are you over there?
Where could you be?
Please don't eat me for your tea.

Giant, giant, could I see you
From England to Ireland?
Giant, giant, can you see me
From Scotland to Wales?

Giant, giant, would you like to come for dinner?
Giant, giant, you need feeding up,
You're looking thinner and thinner.

Giant, giant, would you like bread and buns?
Giant, giant, don't worry,
I have tons and tons.

Giant, giant, please say yes,
I can't wait for you to be my guest.

Lewis Martins (10)
Townsend Primary School, London

Daydream

Miss Billsdon thinks I'm reading, but no . . .
I'm riding with kangaroos
Or jumping in a pool of Coke.
I'm on Mars with my best friends.
I'm a popular footballer.
I'm the richest person ever.

Miss Billsdon thinks I'm listening, but no . . .
I'm dancing with Michael Jackson
Or I'm a twin with Britney Spears.
I'm with a shiny, blue dolphin.
I'm in Tunisia with the Arsenal team.

Holly Flynn (8)
Townsend Primary School, London

What Should I Have For Dinner?

What should I have for dinner?
Should I have chicken?
In the kitchen
Munching rice
With a mice
Chew a chip
With my long, wet lip
Taking big bites of pie
In the desert where it's dry
Sucking spaghetti
On the settee
Eating roast beef and peas
At the Chinese
The more I eat, I get so fat
I'm so fat now, I look like an enormous cat.

Halima Brown (9)
Townsend Primary School, London

Harvest Time

Some people have very little
Some have very much
Give what you can
Share what you've got
One time, harvest was all fruit and crops
Now it is everything from coats to socks
Eyes say thank you, no words are needed
We do not want socks
Just a smile to know we have helped.

Oliver O'Connor (10)
Townsend Primary School, London

Hallowe'en

Hallowe'en
Hallowe'en
Where have you been?
I'm coming round
Maybe for a pound
Where have you been
My sweet Hallowe'en?
Either for some sweets
Or some treats
For a cat
Or a bat
Maybe for a talking hat.
Hallowe'en
Hallowe'en
Where have you been
My sweet Hallowe'en?

Ashley Atkin (10)
Townsend Primary School, London

The Sea

This is the sea,
Billowing like me.
These are the waves,
Rushing as fast as my mum.
This is the rain,
Crying with my sister.
This is the sun,
Light as my dad.

Haja Sesay (10)
Townsend Primary School, London

Harvest

Harvest, harvest, what a wonderful thing,
All the crops to be grown.
A field with corn
With the blazing sun looking down on the field.
The wheat ready to be picked
And full of goodness.
I like sweetcorn, I like wheat,
That's why I like the harvest.

Kelly Thomas (10)
Townsend Primary School, London

Poverty And Hope

Walking barefoot
Dusty, long road
Food for my mum

Discovering new medicine
In a dark, dusty room
Looking forward to making people better

Having pots of drink
Dirty water
Drinking water

Bananas are heavy
Back to my boy
Carrying home

Going to a football match
In a dusty place
Hope my team wins

Eating food
One meal a day
Glad to eat dinner.

Emily Roestenburg (7)
Trinity CE VA First School, Verwood

Poverty And Hope

Writing a long story
Two pairs of clothes
Lots of love

Drinking cold water
No taps or kitchen
Taking water to her mum

Locked water pipe
Not sharing
Have water

Eating spaghetti
Hardly any good
Have joy.

Isabelle Baker (7)
Trinity CE VA First School, Verwood

Poverty And Hope

No water running
Locked up water
Soon open

No home in a big city
No food
Can't sleep

One meal a week
Only meal
Some food

Can't write
No school
Always with friends.

Benjamin Roberts (8)
Trinity CE VA First School, Verwood

Poverty And Hope

Sleeping on a rock
Do not have shelter
Still happy

Writing homework
Cannot do it
Friends to help

Eating food
Only one meal
Have food

Drinking hot water
Don't have tap
Saving some for home

Locked up tap
Cannot share
Still have water.

Chelsie Taylor (7)
Trinity CE VA First School, Verwood

Poverty And Hope

Eating long spaghetti
Only one meal a day
But I am really happy

Thinking what to write
A hard time at school
I've thought what to write

Sleeping on a seat
Nowhere to live
Now living in a city.

Rebecca Foot (7)
Trinity CE VA First School, Verwood

Poverty And Hope

Selling newspapers
Only seven
Earning some money

Making medicine
In a dark room
Saving people

Drinking milk
From coconuts
Quenching thirst

Not enough food
Too many people
Maybe there will be more

Carrying heavy sacks
Backache
Help from America.

Brandon Raggett (8)
Trinity CE VA First School, Verwood

Poverty And Hope

Carrying heavy bananas
Miles to walk
Food for everyone

Carrying bunches of tins
Heavy, heavy tins
Lovely bread

Working as hard as they can
Thinking as hard as they can
Finished at last.

George Nelson (7)
Trinity CE VA First School, Verwood

Poverty And Hope

Giving out newspapers
Only seven
Earning money

Carrying heavy bananas
Lots of bunches
People will help

Having snack
One meal only
Happy and full up

Not enough clothes
Not enough smiling
Presents filled to the top

Carrying heavy sacks
Bad aching back
Everyone cares about him

Making new medicine
In a small, dark room
Working for money.

Ryan Lilly (7)
Trinity CE VA First School, Verwood

Poverty And Hope

Selling papers all day
Aching hands
Kind people pay

Taking a rest
Feeling tired
Eyes are shutting

Standing in a crowd
In a very hot place
Praising for happiness.

Hannah Stammers (7)
Trinity CE VA First School, Verwood

Poverty And Hope

Working together
Very hard
Learning new things

Spinning water
Locked away
Better to share

Sleeping on a bench
Going to get wet
Not too hot

Eating bread
All gone
Very yummy

Walking together
In a crowd
Never alone

Selling papers
Very hard
Getting money

Drinking milk
No more
But I like it.

Eating spaghetti
One meal
Very yummy

Walking over a road
Very dusty
Walking to freedom

Eating bread
Very dry
But very good

Making new medicine
Aching brains
Helping other people

Carrying heavy sacks
Aching back
People care

Cooking cabbage stew
Very hot
But lovely to eat.

Nathaniel Bellingham Mills (7)
Trinity CE VA First School, Verwood

Poverty And Hope

Smiley face
In a small room
Eating spaghetti

Smiling because of a present
Don't always get presents
Present this Christmas

Good water
Not enough
Grateful for it

Working hard
Backache
For poor people

Long journey
Walking far
Getting food

Washing herself
Thirsty
Drinking water

Lots of people
Squashed
From different countries.

Christopher Hornsby (7)
Trinity CE VA First School, Verwood

Poverty And Hope

Experimenting with medicine
Because it's killing people
Finally found out what it was

Eating food with fingers
Haven't had food for months
Having food now

Crowding around
Too many people
Telling people about God

Selling newspapers
Only seven years old
Getting some money

Carrying heavy sacks
Aching back
Getting money.

Sophie Vandersluys (7)
Trinity CE VA First School, Verwood

Poverty And Hope

Drinking salt water
Only water pipe
For the whole family

Writing small amounts of poetry
Only writing book
They share together

Sleeping quietly
Outside, unsafe, danger
Away from jungle

Locked water pipe
Does not know how to share
Have to use river.

Harvey Appleby (7)
Trinity CE VA First School, Verwood

Poverty And Hope

Drinking cold water
From an open pipe
Water for her family

Big, busy crowd
Too squashed to get home
Glad to be going home

Pipe locked up
Got poison in it
Safe from the poison

Sleeping on a stone
Too hard to sleep
Dreaming of a house

Eating food
First they've tasted
Love food.

Olivia Mitchell (7)
Trinity CE VA First School, Verwood

Poverty And Hope

Crowding together
Huge family
So much love

Sipping water
Always thirsty
Strong drink

Carrying on his back
Sacks full of food
For Mum and family.

Cherice Applegate (7)
Trinity CE VA First School, Verwood

Poverty And Hope

Carrying heavy sacks
Aching back
People care

Selling newspaper
Wish I was playing

People eating
One meal a day
Having more food

Making up a book
Practising hard
Writing

Having a drink of water
Need a towel
Dry myself

People crowding around
Everyone happy
To learn new languages.

Melissa Hall (7)
Trinity CE VA First School, Verwood

Poverty And Hope

Children eating happily
Not very nice food
Thinking it is good

Drinking water
Very dirty
Feeling very happy

Cleaning teeth
Doesn't feel happy
Bubbles round her mouth.

Sophie Mylius (7)
Trinity CE VA First School, Verwood

Poverty And Hope

Drinking water
Low on water
Grateful for it

Dirty house
Broken house
Grateful for it

Drinking Coke
Cooking
Grateful for food

Carrying bags
Heavy bags
Grateful for grain

Thinking what it could be
Working hard
Teachers at school

Large crowd
Gathering for prayer
Never alone.

Charlie Philpot (7)
Trinity CE VA First School, Verwood

Poverty And Hope

Sleeping on a rock bench
No home and no family
Home and family

Eating from a plastic table
Not enough food
More clothes for wearing

Testing a new experiment
Window has no glass
Better home to work.

Chloe Branagan-Liddy (7)
Trinity CE VA First School, Verwood

Poverty And Hope

Drinking milk
Sore fingers
Tasty milk

Opening present
Hard to open
Chocolatey things

Marching dust
Getting cold
Hope to get warmer

Sitting next to buckets
Dirty seat
Comfy seat

Drinking water
Getting cold
Lots of clothes

Eating food
Squashed
Tasty food.

Hayden Griffin (7)
Trinity CE VA First School, Verwood

Poverty And Hope

Thinking girls
No shoes to wear
Love to learn

Opening heavy presents
Not many
Love from others

Carrying heavy sacks
Backache
Taking to another country.

Lauren Gower (7)
Trinity CE VA First School, Verwood

Poverty And Hope

Walking on the dusty road
Hurting his feet
To a new camp

Carrying lots of bananas
Hurting her back
To the shop

Making money
I only sold one
I have sold all of them.

Abigail Lilly (7)
Trinity CE VA First School, Verwood

Poverty And Hope

Shining pots
No money
Food for my family

Carrying bananas
Backache
Food for my family

Locked tap
Other people's water
Another tap.

Charlie Whitehead (8)
Trinity CE VA First School, Verwood

Poverty And Hope

Carrying heavy sacks
Bad backache
Help from Australia

Selling big pots
Too hot to work
Earning money

Making new medicine
In a small, dark room
Making people better

Drinking water
Small room
Having a good drink

Selling newspapers
Only seven
Earning money

Eating food
Dark room
Having noodles

Walking through the desert
Away from war
Safe away from war.

Sam Spencer (7)
Trinity CE VA First School, Verwood

Poverty And Hope

No drinking water
Belongs to someone else
Bring some to me

Carrying heavy bananas
Backache from the work
Food for my family

Walking away from war
Left the home away
Come back one day.

Sophie Wilkinson (7)
Trinity CE VA First School, Verwood

Autumn

Trees dancing,
Leaves flying,
Flowers drooping,
Birds cheeping,
Conkers clonking,
Twigs rolling,
Rivers rushing,
Grass swaying,
Dogs barking,
Rabbits hopping.

Harry Foster (7)
Westbourne Primary School, Westbourne

The Wind

The wind is really fast.
The wind is blowing the leaves away.
The wind is whistling like a ghost.
The wind is whooshing the women's hats in the park.
The wind is blowing hard.
The wind is rattling.
The wind is very strong, it can blow a man over.
The wind is making the people feel cold.
The wind is whistling at night-time.
The wind is making the leaves rattle.
The wind is undying.
The wind is swishing.
The wind is very soft.
The wind is very windy.
The wind is very noisy.

Sarah Ayob (8)
William Patten School, London

Naughty Wind

As the wind goes all over the world it never stops.
It would give you a rest for two or three days.
It would come back and bring a lot of rain and become freezing.
As the wind goes by, it blows you and something of yours blows.
As it is so cold, it would become smoky and you cannot see anything.
Have you ever seen the wind?
I haven't and I think no one has.
As the wind is so strong, it can break leaves.
The leaves can blow in your face, not just one but two or three.
At night the wind is gentle and wandering around.
As you are in your bed you can hear the wind.
It sounds like a spooky monster coming to eat you.

Aysha Kola (8)
William Patten School, London

Luc's Feelings

The wind sounds like . . .
A mouse crawling on the floor,
An ant walking around,
The wind whispering,
A cat purring,
A puppy barking,
A kitten miaowing,
A boy napping,
A ghost whistling,
An alien listening,
A big brass band,
But to me the wind feels like my mum is next to me.

Luc Neave (8)
William Patten School, London

The Wind

The wind travels round the world giving people grief,
When the sun comes out, it gives a sigh of relief.

When the wind proudly rushes around,
It shows annoyance to the people down in the town.

When it's night you can hear a wolf call,
When it's night you can hear a royal ball.

When it's day you can hear a parrot squawk,
When day is through the wind acts time and again like gale force.

When there is a hurricane you can't explain.

When there is a tornado don't let your kids use Play-Doh.
Run into a place where there is space
And don't be in a place where there is no space.

Louis Kirby (8)
William Patten School, London

The Wind

Could you hear a dog groaning in the wind?
Could you feel the wind whizzing through the trees?
Can you hear a hurricane whistling through the Earth?
Can you hear a werewolf howling in the breeze?
The spooky branches touching the gale.
Can you hear the wind crying through the town?
Can you see the wind passing by your house?
Can you hear the wind turning into a superhero?

Noor Mohammed (9)
William Patten School, London

The Wind

The wind has come,
The house flew away.
The wind has come,
The bird flies away.
The wind has come,
The hat flew away.
The wind has come.
Please go away.

Sayam Saensri (9)
William Patten School, London

Untitled

The trees sway,
The leaves fly away.
The umbrellas pop in and out,
The tree flies away,
The leaves fly away,
The hat flies away.
The rubbish fluttering away.
The wind is blowing by the house.
The wind is wild over the farm.

Paramjeet Kaur (8)
William Patten School, London

The Gift Of Wind

The wind sounds so strong
As if it's in a song.

The wind crackles in the sea
As loud as it can be.

The wind is like a ghost
Dancing on toast.

The wind is very swift
Almost like a gift.

The wind is like a dog growling
Or a cat prowling.

From time to time
The wind will climb.

The wind blows away the eggs
And rustles in the clothes' pegs.

Felix Jenkins (8)
William Patten School, London

The Whistling Wind

The wind is whispering all through the night,
Like it's in a gigantic fight.
The wind is blowing,
The wind is whistling,
The wind is spooky.
What was that?
A ghost whispering,
An alien listening,
An owl moaning?
Oh, it's just the wind.
It's just the wind.

Joseph Walker (8)
William Patten School, London

The Pushing Wind

One night the wind came through the windows
And ruined ten games of bingo.
The wind passed the haunted house
And frightened away the little mouse.
The wind killed all the hair lice
And followed the baby mice.
The wind pushed a rat to sleep
And did not take one single peep.
The wind pushed a little girl to her home,
The wind blew a dead fish's bone.

Sophie Kouznetsova (8)
William Patten School, London

Wind Poem

Cold wind, stormy wind, breezy wind, draughty wind.
The wind is blowing
And when the sun comes out the wind is angry.
The wind is passing through and the wind is crying.
I said, 'Don't cry.'
The next morning it's cold and the wind is making it colder.
When the cold wind is finished, it is sunny but cold.
The wind is trembling and it's a nice day.

Zayhadar Sayad (8)
William Patten School, London

Horrible Wind

The wind is killing the baby rats
And covers them with a spiky mat.
The wind is passing the haunted house
And frightens a baby mouse.
The wind is pushing the plants,
They did not have a chance.

Kacey-Ann Hibbert (8)
William Patten School, London

Worldwide Wind

The wind is very strong,
Crashing and diving all over the place,
All over the world.
It is throwing up cars, lorries, buildings,
Everything in its way.
Can you stop it?
I don't think so.
Maybe in later years we can,
But it's not very likely.
When the wind comes,
It leaves its mark.
It is basically here every day,
Swirling and gliding around.
Sometimes fast and sometimes slow,
Whenever it comes, you will know.

Theo Barber-Bany (8)
William Patten School, London

The Brainstorm

Oh wind, why do you go around the Earth?
Because I like doing brainstorming,
Seeing children playing so many other different games.
Do you know that you're wrecking the Earth
When you have so much fun?
I don't see what I'm doing.
Wrecking the houses when you go past.
Trees falling on the ground and cars flying away,
People and birds flying away.
That's what you're doing.
When you get really angry, you make a tornado,
So be careful, keep your temper down
And do gentle winds instead.
Then everyone in the whole world
Will like you very much.

Tahmid Khan (8)
William Patten School, London

The Wind

A mouse crawling on the floor.
The strong wind.
The swift wind.
The annoying wind.
The stormy wind.
The breezy wind.
A ghost whistling.
The door knocking.
A wolf howling.
A bird tweeting.
I like the wind because it blows the heat away from the sun.

Antoine Hudson (8)
William Patten School, London

The Wind

The wind blows like a person,
The wind is fast like a race,
The wind is making everything move like a tornado,
The wind is lonely and slow,
The wind is rattling like rain,
The wind blows the scarf off your face,
The wind is annoying when it blows your hair,
The wind is breezy like cold, not hot weather,
The wind is soft as a person,
The wind is whistling like a ghost in the sky,
The wind blows fast,
The wind blows the trees down.

Juwairia Yunus (8)
William Patten School, London

Moods Of The Wind

The wind so soothing,
The wind so loud.

At night the wind comes to a stop,
Then in the morning the wind fades away.

When it snows the wind is glad,
But when it goes the wind is sad.

The wind can be spooky,
The wind can be fun.

At night the wind is like a ghost
And that's what it's like to me.

Molly O'Donovan-Cudsi (8)
William Patten School, London

Sound By Wind

One night it was quiet, silent and still,
I could see the moon shining, on a grassy hill.
I could hear a banshee howling into the dark,
I could hear waves crashing and the sound of a shark.
And as the night turns into dawn,
The wind whispers secrets into the ears of a fawn.
And as the light just starts to appear, the air is fit to freeze,
But exactly one hour later that day, comes a calm summer breeze.

Rakhi Biswas Evans (8)
William Patten School, London

What The Wind Does

As the wind goes by, it blows in your face,
It's like lightning in its own pace.
You never ever see the wind because it's whirling around,
That's why it has no sound.
Far away in the rustling trees,
There is a man on his knees.
That man is so bare,
He has no hair.
Then so quickly there is a sound
Of a gust of wind with a pound.
As the wind goes by,
A feather lands on a man's thigh.
Whoosh through the night,
It gives me a fright.
Have you ever wondered what life's about?
The wind will figure it out.

Kezia Lenton (8)
William Patten School, London

The Wind

I can see ice in the wind,
I can see cats dancing in the wind,
I can see birds flying through the wind.
The wind blew my hat away,
Umbrellas turn inside out,
The leaves come off the trees.

Jordan Rhoden-Thomas (8)
William Patten School, London

Night And Day

The wind is like a ghost whistling through the night,
It rattles the trees and drops the leaves,
It cackles away,
When morning comes it swiftly moves out of the day.
The breeze says goodbye,
Then says hi to everybody around it, how nice.
When it's night again, the wind taps at my window,
It cries very softly and whispers to me.
The next day it's dull and cold.
My dad is in bed.
He says it's too cold to go anywhere.
He's right of course, it's freezing.
I can see my breath outside.
I run straight back in the house.
It's too cold, just too cold.
The night is dull and dingy, just like the day.
I don't know why, do you?

Hannah Verdon (8)
William Patten School, London